Little Offices of the Passion

Little Offices of the Passion

by
St. Bonaventure of Bagnoregio
and
St. Francis of Assisi

IN SIDE-BY-SIDE LATIN AND ENGLISH

PO Box 217 | St. Marys, KS 66536

Library of Congress Control Number: 2024038088

© 2025 by Angelus Press
All rights reserved.

ANGELUS PRESS
PO Box 217
Saint Marys, Kansas 66536
Phone (816) 753-3150
FAX (816) 753-3557
Order Line 1-800-966-7337
www.angeluspress.org

ISBN: 978-1-68529-080-1
FIRST PRINTING–February 2025

Printed by Brilliant Printers, Bengaluru, India

Go out, O daughter of Sion, and behold the glory of Solomon: the steed He rides, the garments and palm branches strewn before Him, the praises that greet Him. How has the flower of Your glory withered so quickly? Your honor has turned to disgrace, Your sweetness to vinegar. You bear the cross on Your shoulders, You are stripped of your garments, flogged with the scourge, filled with reproaches, driven out of the city. Behold the wisdom of our Solomon regarding the time of His death: He suffered on the sixth hour of the sixth day of the week, so that by His death He might restore life to humanity, who fell at this hour on this day.

*Meditation on the Sufferings of Our Lord
of anonymous medieval authorship**

---

* Excerpted by Ludolph of Saxony in *The Life of Jesus Christ, Part II*, vol. 2, trans. Milton T. Walsh (Collegeville, Minnesota: Liturgical Press, 2022), chapter 67, p. 349.

The Arrest of Jesus
Philadelphia, Free Library of Philadelphia, 1945-65-4 (Collins Hours), fol. 13v.

CONTENTS

Introduction 1

St. Bonaventure's Little Office of the Passion

Matins 11
Lauds 21
Prime 29
Terce 35
Sext 41
None 47
Vespers 53
Compline 61

Antiphons to the Blessed Virgin Mary

Alma Redemptóris Mater 69, 74
Ave, Regína cælórum 70, 76
Regína cæli 71, 78
Salve Regína 72, 79
Sub tuum præsídium 73, 82

St. Francis's Little Office of the Passion

Ordinary 85
Propers 92

The Passion of Our Lord Jesus Christ According to

St. John 125
St. Luke 137
St. Matthew 147
St. Mark 159

The Seven Penitential Psalms 168

ILLUSTRATIONS

The Arrest of Jesus.......................... vi
1945-65-4 (Collins Hours), fol. 13v.
The Scourging at the Pillar 10
1945-65-4 (Collins Hours), fol. 15v.
The Crowning with Thorns................... 20
1945-65-13, p. 221.
The Judging before Pilate 28
1945-65-13, p. 218.
The Carrying of the Cross 34
1945-65-4 (Collins Hours), fol. 17v.
The Crucifixion.............................. 40
1945-65-13, p. 227.
The Deposition 46
1945-65-13, p. 230.
The Harrowing of Hell 52
1945-65-4 (Collins Hours), fol. 24v.
The Entombment 60
1945-65-4 (Collins Hours), fol. 20v.
The Pietà.................................... 68
1945-65-13, p. 48.
St. Francis Receiving the Stigmata 84
Lewis E 113, fol. 59v.
St. John 124
1945-65-4 (Collins Hours), fol. 27v.
St. Luke.................................... 136
1945-65-4 (Collins Hours), fol. 29v.
St. Matthew................................. 146
1945-65-4 (Collins Hours), fol. 32v.
St. Mark 158
1945-65-4 (Collins Hours), fol. 35v.

ON THE IMAGES USED

THE images used in this modern Book of Hours are reused, in true medieval fashion, from three medieval Books of Hours all held in Philadelphia and hosted by the BiblioPhilly open-access digital repository. They are known by their shelfmarks, listed below:

- 1945-65-4 (Collins Hours) (c. 1445-1450, Bruges or Flanders)
- 1945-65-13 (c. 1400-1600, France)
- Lewis E 113 (c. 1400-1600, Paris)

Of these three, we have primarily used images from the first two: the brilliant work of the Collins Master has been interspersed with illuminations from another Passion sequence where images in the Collins Hours were lacking or had been removed over the centuries (likely cut out and sold to furnish some other manuscript, now lost, or kept for personal devotion, just as we have done here—notably without the detriment, however, to the original).

The recurring Tau cross motif, inspired by a drawing done in St. Francis's own hand, and the praises of God juxtaposed with it, are taken from a page written by St. Francis immediately after his reception of the stigmata; the original manuscript is held at the Sacro Convento at Assisi and is known now as the Chartula.

The Passion sequence we have created here, which corresponds to the hours in St. Bonaventure's and St. Francis's offices, has been supplemented by an image of St. Francis from the third manuscript.

The marbled endpapers in this twenty-first-century edition are reproduced from the eighteenth-century binding on a fifteenth-century French translation of a thirteenth-century Bible, designated by the library record as Widener 2, also held in Philadelphia.

We thank the Free Library of Pennsylvania for making these images accessible in the public domain, and we are privileged to place them in a setting here that allows them to be used once more for devotion and contemplation, as their makers so long ago intended.

ON THE EDITIONS USED

WE have compiled these texts from the editions listed below with only small modifications. To St. Bonaventure's Office, which is standard in form, we have added the normal features of an Office which the original editors omitted for the sake of presenting what was most clearly St. Bonaventure's own work in his *Opera Omnia*. We have also updated the translations of several antiphons to make them better match the Latin text. For St. Francis's Office, we have made slight adjustments to update the Latin and English according to the most recent scholarship. All English Scripture translations are taken from the Douay-Rheims translation.

St. Bonaventure, *Officium de passione Domini*, in *Doctoris Seraphici S. Bonaventurae opera omnia*, vol. 8 of 10, *Opuscula varia ad theologiam mysticam, et res Ordinis Fratrum Minorum spectantia,* 152–158 (Quaracchi: Collegium S. Bonaventurae, 1898).

St. Bonaventure, *Little Office of the Passion* (Chicago: Franciscan Herald Press, undated).

St. Francis of Assisi, *Opuscula Sancti Patris Francisci Assisiensis* (Quaracchi: Collegium S. Bonaventurae, 1904).

St. Francis of Assisi, Part III of *The Writings of Francis of Assisi,* trans. Paschal Robinson, (Philadelphia: The Dolphin Press, 1906).

INTRODUCTION

THE saints of the Church have often produced aids for those desiring to grow in devotion to Our Lord, especially to his Passion; and while the saints have employed many different genres to inform devotion to Christ, there is perhaps none greater than the devotion offered in a liturgical Office. This little book, which presents two of these Offices by two of the great saints of the Church, is what medieval men and women would have called a Book of Hours. Time back then was marked liturgically both throughout the year and throughout each day: church bells rang the canonical hours and clerics gathered, with laity often assisting, to sing the perpetual prayer of the Church. The Office, like the Mass and its Propers, proceeds by certain formulae and with certain expectations: hymns, antiphons, and prayers surround the chosen psalms as a setting frames a jewel; and the jewels of the psalms themselves are chosen to adorn and illuminate, in particular and meaningful ways, the thoughts of the Church. The highest form of praise sung to God daily is given by arranging His own inspired words beautifully for each occasion, because none can be more fitting than those the Divine Author has provided about Himself; and man's co-creation in arranging those words is like that of a fine craftsman, shaping delicate golden figures around brilliant truths, to be presented again to the Father.

The ubiquity of the Office in the Middle Ages meant that devotional creativity was often channeled through this familiar form to honor certain personages or events—either for a feast-day, for a feast octave, or for the daily commemoration of some mystery of the Church. It is these types of

shorter daily Offices which are customarily found in Books of Hours designed for lay devotional use. The most popular of these "Little Offices" was that of the Blessed Virgin Mary, but other offices were often included alongside it—the Office of the Dead, the Office of the Cross, the Office of the Holy Spirit, or an Office of the Passion as we have here (or perhaps two or three of the above in combination). St. Francis is known to have said the Church's Office, the Little Office of the Blessed Virgin, and his own Office of the Passion every day. The Gospel accounts of the Passion and the penitential psalms, included here, were common addenda to Books of Hours.

Within the familiar strictures of the Mass and the Office, as with the fixed form of a sonnet, comes a remarkable freedom to give voice to the entire devotional range of the Church, and the entire emotional range of man. Offices dedicated to the Passion commemorate Christ's suffering by connecting specific hours of prayer to the moments of His Passion: the Crucifixion, for example, was always remembered at the hour of Sext.

St. Bonaventure and St. Francis of Assisi were particularly suited to produce rich texts for devotional prayer on the Passion, for the former obtained the highest level of theological education available at the time, and the latter received the marks of the Passion in a mystical vision. In what follows, we provide first a very brief introduction to the circumstances that occasioned each Office and its form, and then some remarks about the texts themselves.

St. Francis of Assisi, who died in 1226, perhaps began composing prayers that would become his Office of the Passion sometime around 1205, when he began to live a more dedicated religious life but had not yet formally become a

religious. To the initial texts of his Office, St. Francis added more and more pieces over the course of his life, until the Office of the Passion assumed the shape it now has sometime before the saint's death. St. Francis's Office has a series of elements, all of which are original to the saint, though they are indebted to or sometimes entirely composed out of the Psalms and other Scriptural texts.

St. Francis's Office does not follow the conventions of a text like the Little Office of the Blessed Virgin. Instead, St. Francis's Office began with an *Our Father*, though the precise prayer may have been Francis's own meditative elongation of the *Our Father* provided here, sometimes referred to as *Exposition of the Our Father*. Following the *Our Father*, St. Francis said the *Glory be*. St. Francis's own composition—*The Praises to Be Said at All Hours*—follows; these are a stirring hymn of praise to God informed by the books of the Apocalypse and Daniel. The *Praises* ask the reader to enter the glorious throne room of St. John's Apocalypse and behold God and the Lamb, and from this height, to invite all of creation to praise and bless God, the creator and savior. With the completion of these praises, St. Francis prayed a unique Collect, whose focus is on God the highest good to whom all praise is due, from whom and to whom all goods flow. Then St. Francis moved on to pray a single original psalm composition for each hour, framed by a Marian antiphon likewise of his own composition. The Marian antiphon invokes our Lady under familiar titles that relate the Mother of God to each of the Trinitarian persons, as she leads the saints and angels in prayer to her Son. The antiphon concludes with a *Glory be*.

The original psalms which make up St. Francis's Office are here designated by roman numerals to distinguish them from those of the Psalter, which are referred to in arabic nu-

merals. We have marked in italics where St. Francis's compositions differ from the Latin found in the Vulgate, both to avoid possible confusion and to highlight his own style and devotion.

The Office concluded with a blessing that echoed the themes of St. Francis's Collect—God as supreme Good, the one who deserves all our praise and from whom all Good derives. We have here also provided another of St. Francis's prayers, the *Salutation of the Blessed Virgin*, to be used as a Marian antiphon after the conclusion of the hour of Compline. While this prayer exists in two separate traditions, the version provided here follows the tradition that scholars argue is closest to what St. Francis said.

St. Bonaventure, who died in 1274, joined the Franciscan order around 1243. Though St. Bonaventure likely never met St. Francis during his life, he was the beneficiary of his intercessory power. Thus, in his Major and Minor Legend of St. Francis, St. Bonaventure acknowledges that he was spared from a childhood illness by his mother's prayers to St. Francis. This memory, and other factors, surely prompted St. Bonaventure to enter the Franciscans, rather than become a diocesan priest or join another mendicant or monastic community. St. Bonaventure became a Master of Philosophy and Theology at Paris around 1243 and 1254 respectively, making him one of the top intellectuals of his day, on par with his contemporary St. Thomas Aquinas. He produced the works expected of a Master of Theology during his tenure as Master between 1254 and 1257: commentaries on Peter Lombard's *Sentences*, commentaries on Scripture, disputed questions, and sermons. In 1257, St. Bonaventure was elected Minister General of the Franciscan order. He served in this capacity into the 1270s, when he was made a Cardinal Bishop. He died in service to the Church at the second

council of Lyons on July 15, 1274. St. Thomas Aquinas had died four months prior.

During St. Bonaventure's lengthy service as Minister General, he traveled Europe governing the order and aiding the hierarchy of the Church. While doing so he codified the Franciscan Order's constitutions, wrote new lives of Saint Francis, and produced theological and devotional works. St. Bonaventure's *Journey of the Mind into God* and *The Tree of Life* may be the most famous of these texts now.

As is often the case, a man of St. Bonaventure's fame was also called upon to produce texts for others. The Franciscans and Dominicans at Paris had developed close ties with the royal court of St. Louis IX. St. Bonaventure preached before the royal family on many occasions, and may have written one of his devotional works, *On Governance of Soul*, for St. Louis IX's daughter Blanche. It is traditionally believed that St. Bonaventure composed the Office of the Passion at the request of St. Louis IX for the royal saint's own use. Because it follows the format of a conventional Office, we have chosen to place St. Bonaventure's Little Office of the Passion first in this volume, since those accustomed to saying the Divine Office or the Little Office of the Blessed Virgin Mary will find it more approachable at first.

The two Offices presented here begin the narrative of the Passion in slightly different places: St. Bonaventure's begins at Matins and Lauds, remembering Christ imprisoned in the early hours of the morning, while St. Francis's Office begins at Compline the night prior by commemorating the Agony in the Garden. Both St. Francis and St. Bonaventure often use the Psalms to speak with Christ's voice, evoking the pathos of each moment. St. Francis speaks with Christ during the hour of the Agony: "My holy Father, King of heaven and

earth, depart not from me: for tribulation is near and there is none to help."

It is noticeable that St. Francis often slightly modifies the words of the Vulgate to express a deep sense of trust in God's fatherhood. While "Holy Father," a frequent interpolation into the texts from the Psalter, is found in the Vulgate on the lips of Christ (Jn. 17:11), St. Francis intensifies and personalizes it: "my most holy Father," as in Psalms II, III, V, and VI. The immense trust in the Father expressed here is only enriched by the knowledge that St. Francis's own father was largely absent from his life after an explosive public dispute over St. Francis's commitment to the life of poverty. That life of strict poverty and instability also stands in itself as an expression of absolute trust in God the Father's loving care.

This element, and other elements in St. Francis's Office, indicate that it is a continuous prayer born out of lifelong devotion for, and constant meditation on, the most fundamental elements of the Catholic faith, learned by every child at his mother's knee: the Our Father, the Hail Mary, the Creed, and the Commandments. We find these simple but inexhaustible elements immeasurably enriched by decades of ferment in St. Francis's memory—from the extended meditation on the Our Father which here prefaces the Office; to the single repeated antiphon saluting Our Lady as she leads the heavenly host in prayer; to the interpolations from the Creed and the Gospels (as in Psalm VII) which deepen and fulfill the verses from the Psalter by referring them to Christ; to the insistent references to God's judgment, justice, and precepts (as in Psalms VI, VII, XI, and XV).

St. Francis held Psalm XV so dear that he repeated it five times daily throughout the Christmas season, and it is a particularly clear window into his devotion. It calls to mind two events his biographer, Thomas of Celano, felt were the most

central to understanding the saint: his live reenactment of the Nativity at Greccio, and his reception of the Stigmata on the mountain of La Verna. It begins with Psalm 80—"Rejoice!"—and continues: "For the most holy Father of heaven, our King before ages, sent His Beloved Son from on high: and he was born of the Blessed Virgin, holy Mary." We then immediately hear the Christ child crying out through the words of Psalm 88: "He shall cry out to me, Thou art my Father: and I will make Him My Firstborn." The prophecy from Isaiah is completed by Luke, and enacted by St. Francis at Greccio: "For the beloved and most holy Child has been given to us and born for us by the wayside: and laid in a manger because He had no room at the inn." But this rejoicing at Christ's birth is intimately tied with the Crucifixion. Psalm XV ends, in words uniquely St. Francis's own, by juxtaposing the gifts brought at Epiphany ("Bring to the Lord, O you kindreds of the gentiles, bring to the Lord glory and honor") with a call to crucifixion, the gift we ultimately bear in ourselves to the Christ child in the manger: "Bring your own bodies and bear His holy cross: and follow his precepts even unto the end." God rewarded St. Francis's devotion, expressed so richly here, by marking the saint with exactly what he prayed for. Two years before his death, St. Francis physically began to physically bear the marks of the holy cross in his own body when he received the Stigmata.

Each hour is not only devotionally and emotionally rich, but doctrinally so as well. In his Office of the Passion, St. Bonaventure, for example, chooses Psalm 29 for Vespers, marking a triumphant break in the Passion narrative by reminding the faithful of Christ's harrowing of Hell, occurring even as his body is removed from the Cross and entombed. The Psalm echoes the cries of those freed: "Thou hast brought forth, O Lord, my soul from hell: Thou hast saved me from

them that go down into the pit…The Lord hath heard, and hath had mercy on me: the Lord became my helper. Thou hast turned for me my mourning into joy: Thou hast cut my sackcloth, and hast compassed me with gladness." The antiphon, "Thou art worthy, O Lord, to take the book and to open the seven seals thereof, because Thou were slain and have redeemed us to God in Thy blood," connects the narrative of Psalm 29 to the final judgment. This one hour presents a microcosm of Catholic eschatology: even on the very day of Christ's death, as his body is taken from the Cross and mourned by his companions, Heaven raises calls of triumph and, outside of time, sounds the trumpets of judgment: for it is by this act, now accomplished, that men are saved. St. Francis's Vespers (Psalm VII) is likewise triumphal, beginning with lines taken from Psalm 46: "O clap your hands, all you nations: shout to God with the voice of joy."

Those familiar with the ordinary of the Latin Mass, which was largely as we know it now long before St. Bonaventure's time, will also notice that St. Bonaventure, himself a priest, has chosen two psalms from the Mass for the hours of Prime and Sext. At the hour of Prime, when Christ is said to have come before Pilate, St. Bonaventure has chosen Psalm 42, *Judica me*, which the priest recites in its entirety either alone or in chorus with a server prior to ascending to the altar. By this choice St. Bonaventure deftly illuminates Christ as priest and the Cross as altar; it is as if the Mass itself has begun in front of Pilate. With poignancy we no longer hear just the priest, but Christ himself, about to suffer and die, saying, "I will go in to the altar of God: to God who giveth joy to my youth." That this confluence of images is likely intentional is compounded by the fact that St. Bonaventure chooses Psalm 115, *Credidi*, for the hour of Sext. In the Mass, this psalm is said immediately after the priest communicates. He says,

"What shall I render to the Lord, for all the things that He hath rendered to me? I will take the chalice of salvation, and I will call upon the name of the Lord." The rest of the psalm, included in full in St. Bonaventure's office, again ties Christ's death on the altar of the cross to the priesthood: "I will pay my vows to the Lord before all His people…I will sacrifice to Thee the sacrifice of praise." The consummation of the Passion in Christ's death at the hour of Sext is linked to the consuming of Our Lord in the unbloody representation of that very same sacrifice.

In the saints we have a "great cloud of witnesses" who urge us to lay aside sin and to focus our eyes on Christ "the author and finisher of the faith" who "endured the cross" and "now sits at the right hand of God" (Heb. 12:1-2). These Offices invite us to enter more deeply into the memory of the Lord's Passion, and more deeply into the devotional lives of St. Francis, St. Bonaventure, and even St. Louis IX. In St. Bonaventure's Office we are taken by a more conventional route into the Passion of Christ. In St. Francis's Office of the Passion, we find a more unique Office composed of texts that invite us into St. Francis's own prayer. The Seraphic Father not only presses us to become more devoted to Christ's suffering; he teaches us to praise God through the created world, to grow in devotion to Our Lady, and to more clearly recognize God as the source of all the goods we have, those of nature gifted to us through creation and those of grace gifted to us by God's redeeming acts, especially Christ's sacrifice on the Cross. Here is how we can better know these saints and, with them, take on the mind of Christ, their Lord and Master: by taking up their prayers daily.

The Scourging at the Pillar
Philadelphia, Free Library of Philadelphia, 1945-65-4 (Collins Hours), fol. 15v.

St. Bonaventure's Little Office of the Passion

Matins

℣. Lord, ✠ thou shalt open my lips.
℟. And my mouth shall declare Thy praise.
℣. O God, ✠ come to my assistance.
℟. O Lord, make haste to help me.
℣. Glory be to the Father, and to the Son, and to the Holy Ghost.
℟. As it was in the beginning, is now, and ever shall be, world without end. Amen. Alleluia.

℣. Dómine, ✠ lábia mea apéries.
℟. Et os meum annuntiábit laudem tuam.
℣. Deus, ✠ in adiutórium meum inténde.
℟. Dómine, ad adiuvándum me festína.
℣. Glória Patri, et Fílio, et Spirítui Sancto.
℟. Sicut erat in princípio, et nunc, et semper, et in sǽcula sæculórum. Amen. Allelúia.

From Septuagesima to Holy Saturday, instead of Alleluia is said:

Praise be to Thee, O Lord, King of glory everlasting.

Laus tibi, Dómine, Rex ætérnæ glóriæ.

INVITATORY

Ant. Christ is captured and put to scorn, scourged and crucified: come, let us adore Him.

Ant. Christum captum et derísum, flagellátum et crucifíxum: veníte adorémus.

PSALM 94 *Venite, exultemus*

COME, let us praise the Lord with joy, let us joyfully sing to God our Savior. Let us come before His presence with thanksgiving, and make a joyful noise to Him with psalms.

Christ is captured and put to scorn, scourged and crucified: come, let us adore Him.

For the Lord is a great God and a great King above all gods, for the Lord will not cast off His people: for in His hand are all the ends of the earth, and the heights of the mountains are His.

Come, let us adore Him.

For the sea is His, and He made it, and His hands formed the dry land. Come let us adore and fall down before God: let us weep before the Lord that made us, for He is the Lord our God; and we are the people of His pasture and the sheep of His hand.

Christ is captured and put to scorn, scourged and crucified: come, let us adore Him.

Today if you shall hear His voice, harden not your hearts, as in the provocation, according to the day of temptation in the wilderness: where your fathers tempted Me, they proved Me, and saw My works.

VENÍTE, exsultémus Dómino, iubilémus Deo, salutári nostro: præoccupémus fáciem eius in confessióne, et in psalmis iubilémus ei.

Christum captum et derísum, flagellátum et crucifixum: veníte adorémus.

Quóniam Deus magnus Dóminus, et Rex magnus super omnes deos, quóniam non repéllet Dóminus plebem suam: quia in manu eius sunt omnes fines terræ, et altitúdines móntium ipsíus sunt.

Veníte adorémus.

Quóniam ipsíus est mare, et ipse fecit illud, et siccam manus eius formavérunt. Veníte, adorémus, et procidámus ante Deum: plorémus coram Dómino, qui fecit nos, quia ipse est Dóminus, Deus noster; nos autem pópulus eius, et oves páscuæ eius.

Christum captum et derísum, flagellátum et crucifixum: veníte adorémus.

Hódie, si vocem eius audiéritis, nolíte obduráre corda vestra, sicut in exacerbatióne secúndum diem tentatiónis in desérto: ubi tentavérunt me patres vestri, probavérunt et vidérunt ópera mea.

St. Bonaventure's Office of the Passion: Matins

Come, let us adore Him.

Forty years long was I offended with that generation, and I said: These always err in heart, and these men have not known My ways: so I swore in My wrath that they shall not enter into My rest.

Christ is captured and put to scorn, scourged and crucified: come, let us adore Him.

Glory be to the Father, and to the Son, and to the Holy Ghost. As it was in the beginning, is now, and ever shall be, world without end. Amen.

Come, let us adore Him.

Ant. Christ is captured and put to scorn, scourged and crucified: come, let us adore Him.

Venite adorémus.

Quadragínta annis próximus fui generatióni huic, et dixi: Semper hi errant corde, ipsi vero non cognovérunt vias meas: quibus iurávi in ira mea; Si introíbunt in réquiem meam.

Christum captum et derísum, flagellátum et crucifíxum: veníte adorémus.

Glória Patri, et Fílio, et Spirítui Sancto. Sicut erat in princípio, et nunc, et semper, et in sǽcula sæculórum. Amen.

Venite adorémus.

Ant. Christum captum et derísum, flagellátum et crucifíxum: veníte adorémus.

HYMN

O may the Passion of the Lord,
Whereby salvation is restored,
The mind with love for Him inspire,
Our solace and our hearts' desire.

In memory let us ever hold
Christ's thorny crown, His pains untold,
The bitter cross whereon He died,
The nails, the lance that pierced His side.

In passióne Dómini,
Qua datur salus hómini,
Sit nostrum refrigérium
Et cordis desidérium.

Portémus in memória,
Dolóres et oppróbria,
Christi corónam spíneam,
Crucem, clavos et lánceam,

And may we constantly recall The reed, the vinegar, the gall, The anguish of that last dread hour, Those sacred wounds whence graces shower.	Et plagas sacratíssimas. Omni laude digníssimas, Acétum, fel, arúndinem Et mortis amaritúdinem.
O may these thoughts our souls imbue With sweetness of celestial dew, Till fostered by His tender care The glorious fruits of grace they bear.	Hæc ómnia nos sátient Et dulcíter inébrient, Nos répleant virtútibus Et gloriósis frúctibus.
O Crucified, we worship Thee, And beg with all our hearts that we May be united through Thy Love With all the saints in heaven above.	Te crucifíxum cólimus Et toto corde póscimus, Ut nos Sanctórum cœtibus Coniúngas in cæléstibus.
To Christ, the Lord of Majesty, Betrayed and sold to set us free, Who suffered on the cruel tree, Be praise and honor endlessly. Amen.	Laus, honor Christo véndito Et sine cause pródito, Mortem passo pro pópulo In áspero patíbulo. Amen.

THE NOCTURN

Ant. Men without mercy rose up against Me, and they spared not My life.

Ant. Insurrexérunt in me viri sine misericórdia, et non pepercérunt ánimæ meæ.

PSALM 2 *Quare fremuerunt*

WHY have the Gentiles raged: and the people devised vain things?

QUARE fremuérunt gentes: et pópuli meditáti sunt inánia?

The kings of the earth stood up, and the princes met together: against the Lord, and against His Christ.

Let us break their bonds asunder: and let us cast away their yoke from us.

He that dwelleth in heaven shall laugh at them: and the Lord shall deride them.

Then shall He speak to them in His anger: and trouble them in His rage.

But I am appointed king by Him over Sion, His holy mountain: preaching His commandment.

The Lord hath said to Me: Thou art My Son, this day I have begotten Thee.

Ask of Me, and I will give Thee the Gentiles for Thy inheritance: and the utmost parts of the earth for Thy possession.

Thou shalt rule them with a rod of iron: and shall break them in pieces like a potter's vessel.

And now, O kings, understand: receive instruction, you that judge the earth.

Serve the Lord with fear: and rejoice unto Him with trembling.

Embrace discipline, lest at any time the Lord be angry: and you perish from the just way.

Astitérunt reges terræ, et príncipes convenérunt in unum: advérsus Dóminum, et advérsus Christum eius.

Dirumpámus víncula eórum: et proiciámus a nobis iugum ipsórum.

Qui hábitat in cælis irridébit eos: et Dóminus subsannábit eos.

Tunc loquétur ad eos in ira sua: et in furóre suo conturbábit eos.

Ego autem constitútus sum Rex ab eo super Sion, montem sanctum eius: prædicans præcéptum eius.

Dóminus dixit ad me: Fílius meus es tu, ego hódie génui te.

Póstula a me, et dabo tibi gentes hæreditátem tuam: et possessiónem tuam términos terræ.

Reges eos in virga férrea: et tamquam vas fíguli confrínges eos.

Et nunc, reges, intellígite: erudímini, qui iudicátis terram.

Servíte Dómino in timóre: et exsultáte ei cum tremóre.

Apprehéndite disciplínam, nequándo irascátur Dóminus: et pereátis de via iusta.

When His wrath shall be kindled in a short time: blessed are they that trust in Him.

Glory be to the Father and to the Son and to the Holy Ghost.

As it was in the beginning, is now, and ever shall be, world without end. Amen.

Ant. Men without mercy rose up against Me, and they spared not My life.

Matins continues with the following versicles.

℣. I have forsaken my house, I have left my inheritance.

℟. I have given my soul into the hands of sinners.

Our Father *(in secret until)*

℣. And lead us not into temptation.

℟. But deliver us from evil.

Absolution

℣. May the Passion of our Lord Jesus Christ bring us to the joys of paradise.

℟. Amen.

Blessing

℣. Pray, Lord, a blessing.

Through His Holy Passion may our Lord grant us His benediction.

℟. Amen.

Cum exárserit in brevi ira eius: beáti omnes qui confídunt in eo.

Glória Patri, et Fílio, et Spirítui Sancto.

Sicut erat in princípio, et nunc, et semper, et in sæcula sæculórum. Amen.

Ant. Insurrexérunt in me viri sine misericórdia, et non pepercérunt ánimæ meæ.

℣. Réliqui domum meam, dimísi hæréditam meam.

℟. Dedi diléctam ánimam meam in manus peccatórum.

Pater noster *(secreto usque ad)*

℣. Et ne nos indúcas in tentatiónem.

℟. Sed líbera nos a malo.

℣. Pássio Dómini nostri Iesu Christi perdúcat nos ad gáudia paradísi.

℟. Amen.

℣. Iube, Dómine, benedícere.

Per suam sanctam passiónem det nobis Dóminus suam benedictiónem.

℟. Amen.

St. Bonaventure's Office of the Passion: Matins

FIRST LESSON *Jn. 19:1-3*

PILATE took Jesus and scourged Him. And the soldiers, plaiting a crown of thorns, put it upon His head: and they put on Him a purple garment. And they came to Him and said: Hail, King of the Jews. And they gave Him blows, and spitting upon Him, they took the reed and struck His head.—But Thou, O Lord, have mercy on us.

℟. Thanks be to God.

℟. The ancients consulted together that by subtlety they might apprehend Jesus and put Him to death. They went out, as it were to a robber, with swords and clubs.

℣. The chief priests and the Pharisees consulted together that by subtlety they might apprehend Jesus and put Him to death. They went out, as it were to a robber, with swords and clubs.

APPREHÉNDIT Pilátus Iesum et flagellávit. Et mílites, plecténtes corónam de spinis, imposuérunt cápiti eius et veste purpúrea circumdedérunt eum. Et veniébant ad eum et dicébant: Ave Rex Iudæórum. Et dabant ei álapas, et exspúentes in eum, accepérunt arúndinem et percutiébant caput eius.—Tu autem, Dómine, miserére nobis.

℟. Deo grátias.

℣. Senióres consílium fecérunt in unum, ut Iesum dolo tenérent et occíderent. Cum gládiis et fústibus exiérunt tanquam ad latrónem.

℟. Collegérunt Pontífices et Pharisǽi consílium, ut Iesum dolo tenérent et occíderent. Cum gládiis et fústibus exiérunt tanquam ad latrónem.

Blessing

℣. Pray, Lord, a blessing.

Through the might of His Holy Cross, may our Lord bring us to the joys of light and truth.

℟. Amen.

℣. Iube, Dómine, benedícere.

Per virtútem sanctæ crucis, perdúcat nos Dóminus ad gáudia veræ lucis.

℟. Amen.

SECOND LESSON *Jn.* 19:16-18; *Lk.* 23:34

BUT the soldiers took Jesus and led Him forth, and bearing His own cross, He went forth to that place which is called Calvary, but in Hebrew Golgotha, where they crucified Him and with Him two others, one on each side, and Jesus in the midst. And Jesus said: Father, forgive them, for they know not what they do.—But Thou, O Lord, have mercy on us.

℟. Thanks be to God.

℟. You are come out, as it were to a robber, with swords and clubs to apprehend Me. Daily I was before you in the temple teaching, and you did not seize Me, and behold, after I was scourged, you took Me out to be crucified.

℣. And when they had laid hands on Jesus and taken Him, He said to them: Daily I was before you in the temple teaching, and you did not seize Me, and behold, after I was scourged, you took Me out to be crucified.

SUSCEPÉRUNT autem mílites Iesum et eduxérunt, et báiulans sibi crucem, exívit in eum, qui dícitur Calváriæ locum, Hebráice autem Gólgotha, ubi crucifixérunt eum, et cum eo álios duos hinc et hinc, médium autem Iesum. Iesus autem dicébat: Pater dimítte illis; non enim sciunt, quid fáciunt.—Tu autem, Dómine, miserére nobis.

℟. Deo grátias.

℟. Tanquam ad latrónem exísti cum gládiis et fústibus comprehéndere me. Quotídie apud vos eram in templo docens, et non tenuístis me, et ecce, flagellátum dúcitis ad crucifigéndum.

℣. Cumque iniecíssent manus in Iesum et tenuíssent eum, dixit ad eos: Quotídie apud vos eram in templo docens, et non tenuístis me, et ecce, flagellátum dúcitis ad crucifigéndum.

Blessing

℣. Pray, Lord, a blessing.
May the sprinkling of Christ's Blood be our everlasting health and protection.

℟. Amen.

℣. Iube, Dómine, benedícere.
Sánguinis Christi aspérsio sit nobis sempitérna salus et protéctio.

℟. Amen.

THIRD LESSON *Jn* 19:28-30

AFTERWARDS, Jesus knowing that all things were now accomplished, that the Scripture might be fulfilled, said: I thirst. Now there was a vessel set there full of vinegar. And they, putting a sponge full of vinegar about hyssop, put it to His mouth. Jesus, therefore, when He had taken the vinegar, said: It is consummated. And bowing His head, He gave up the ghost.— But Thou, O Lord, have mercy on us.

℟. Thanks be to God.

℟. Darkness covered the earth, whilst the Jews crucified Jesus. And about the ninth hour, Jesus cried out with a loud voice: My God, my God, why has thou forsaken Me? And bowing down His head, He gave up the ghost.

℣. Jesus crying out with a loud voice, said: Father, into thy hands I commend my spirit. And bowing down His head, He gave up the ghost.

℟. Glory be to the Father, and to the Son, and to the Holy Ghost.

℣. And bowing down His head, He gave up the ghost.

POSTEA sciens Iesus, qui ómnia consummáta sunt, ut implerétur Scriptúra, dixit: Sítio. Vas ergo erat pósitum acéto plenum. Illi autem spóngiam plenam acéto hyssópo circumponéntes, obtulérunt ori eius. Cum ergo accepísset Iesus acétum, dixit: Consummátum est, et inclináto cápite, trádidit spíritum.—Tu autem, Dómine, miserére nobis.

℟. Deo grátias.

℟. Ténebræ factæ sunt, dum crucifixíssent Iesum Iudǽi. Et circa horam nonam exclamávit Iesus voce magna: Deus meus, Deus meus, ut quid dereliquísti me? Et inclináto cápite, emísit spíritum.

℣. Exclámans Iesus voce magna, ait: Pater, in manus tuas comméndo spíritum meum.

Et inclináto cápite, emísit spíritum.

℟. Glória Patri, et Fílio, et Spirítui Sancto.

℣. Et inclináto cápite, emísit spíritum.

The Crowning with Thorns

Philadelphia, Free Library of Philadelphia, 1945-65-13, p. 221.

Lauds

℣. O God, ✠ come to my assistance.

℟. O Lord, make haste to help me.

℣. Glory be to the Father, and to the Son, and to the Holy Ghost.

℟. As it was in the beginning, is now, and ever shall be, world without end. Amen. Alleluia.

Ant. Reproaches and terrors have I suffered at their hands, and the Lord is with Me as a mighty warrior.

℣. Deus, ✠ in adiutórium meum inténde.

℟. Dómine, ad adiuvándum me festína.

℣. Glória Patri, et Fílio, et Spirítui Sancto.

℟. Sicut erat in princípio, et nunc, et semper, et in sǽcula sæculórum. Amen. Allelúia.

Ant. Contumélias et terróres passus sum ab eis, et Dóminus mecum est tanquam bellátor fortis.

PSALM 12 *Usquequo, Domine*

How long, O Lord, wilt Thou forget me unto the end? How long dost Thou turn away from me?

How long shall I take counsels in my soul: sorrow in my heart all the day?

How long shall my enemy be exalted over me? Consider, and hear me, O Lord my God.

Enlighten my eyes that I never sleep in death: lest at any time my enemy say, I have prevailed against him.

Usquequo, Dómine, obliviscéris me in finem? Úsquequo avértis fáciem tuam a me?

Quámdiu ponam consília in ánima mea: dolórem in corde meo per diem?

Úsquequo exaltábitur inimícus meus super me? Réspice, et exáudi me, Dómine Deus meus.

Illúmina óculos meos, ne unquam obdórmiam in morte: nequándo dicat inimícus meus, Præválui advérsus eum.

They that trouble me rejoice when I am moved: but I have trusted in Thy mercy.

My heart shall rejoice in Thy salvation: I will sing to the Lord, who giveth me good things: I will sing to the name of the Lord most High.

Glory be to the Father and to the Son and to the Holy Ghost.

As it was in the beginning, is now, and ever shall be, world without end. Amen.

Ant. Reproaches and terrors have I suffered at their hands, and the Lord is with Me as a mighty warrior.

Qui tríbulant me exsultábunt si motus fúero: ego autem in misericórdia tua sperávi.

Exsultábit cor meum in salutári tuo: cantábo Dómino qui bona tríbuit mihi, et psallam nómini Dómini altíssimi.

Glória Patri, et Fílio, et Spirítui Sancto.

Sicut erat in princípio, et nunc, et semper, et in sǽcula sæculórum. Amen.

Ant. Contumélias et terróres passus sum ab eis, et Dóminus mecum est tanquam bellátor fortis.

Capitulum

℣. The breath of our mouth, Christ the Lord, is taken in our sins, to whom we said: under thy shadow we shall live among the Gentiles.

℟. Thanks be to God.

℣. Spíritus oris nostri, Christus Dóminus, captus est in peccátis nostris, cui díximus: in umbra tua vivémus in géntibus.

℟. Deo grátias.

HYMN

Now let us all with one accord
To Christ our Captain anthems raise,
Whose conquering cross our life restored,
Let heaven resound with songs of praise.

Christum ducem, qui per crucem
Redémit nos ab hóstibus
Laudet cœtus noster lætus
Exsúltet cælum láudibus.

O may Thy dreadful agony With true contrition rend our breast, And make us ever seek for Thee, O Jesus, our Redeemer blest.	Pœna fortis tuæ mortis Et sánguinis effúsio Corda terant, ut te quærant, Iesu, nostra redémptio.
Those blissful scars which Jesus bore, The spitting, scourging, buffeting, To us have won forevermore The eternal gifts of Christ our King.	Per felíces cicatríces, Sputa, flagélla, vérbera, Nobis grata sunt colláta ætérna Christi múnera.
Let not Thy Blood be shed in vain But to our hearts its power apply, And wash them clean from every stain, Creator of the starry sky.	Nostrum tangat cor, ut plangat, Tuórum sanguis vúlnerum, In quo toti simus loti, Cónditor alme síderum.
The gifts from which Thy Passion flow Grant us, O Savior, of Thy grace, And in Thy faithfulness bestow The heavenly vision of Thy face.	Passiónis tuæ donis, Salvátor, nos inébria, Qua fidélis dare velis Beáta nobis gáudia.
To Christ, the Lord of Majesty, Betrayed and sold to set us free, Who suffered on the cruel tree, Be praise and honor endlessly. Amen.	Laus, honor Christo véndito Et sine causa pródito, Mortem passo pro pópulo In áspero patíbulo. Amen.

℣. He gave his cheek to him that struck him.

℟. He was filled with reproaches.

℣. Dedit percutiénti se maxíllam.

℟. Saturátus est oppróbriis.

Ant. God spared not His own Son, but delivered Him up for all.

Ant. Próprio Fílio suo non pepércit Deus, sed pro nobis ómnibus trádidit illum.

CANTICLE OF ZACHARY   *Lk.* 1:68-80

BLESSED ✠ be the Lord God of Israel: because He hath visited and wrought the redemption of His people.

And hath raised up a horn of salvation to us: in the house of David His servant.

As He spoke by the mouth of His holy prophets: who are from the beginning.

Salvation from our enemies: and from the hand of all that hate us.

To perform mercy to our fathers: and to remember His holy testament.

The oath which He swore to Abraham our father: that He could grant to us,

That being delivered from the hands of our enemies: we may serve Him without fear,

In holiness and justice before Him: all our days.

And Thou, Child, shalt be called the Prophet of the Highest: for Thou shalt go before the face of the Lord to prepare His ways:

To give knowledge of salvation to His people: unto the remission of their sins;

BENEDÍCTUS ✠ Dóminus Deus Israël: quia visitávit, et fecit redemptiónem plebis suæ.

Et eréxit cornu salútis nobis: in domo David púeri sui.

Sicut locútus est per os sanctórum: qui a sǽculo sunt, prophetárum eius.

Salútem ex inimícis nostris: et de manu ómnium qui odérunt nos.

Ad faciéndam misericórdiam cum pátribus nostris: et memorári testaménti sui sancti.

Iusiurándum quod iurávit ad Ábraham patrem nostrum: datúrum se nobis,

Ut sine timóre, de manu inimicórum nostrórum liberáti: serviámus illi,

In sanctitáte et iustítia coram ipso: ómnibus diébus nostris.

Et tu, puer, Prophéta Altíssimi vocáberis: præíbis enim ante fáciem Dómini paráre vias eius.

Ad dandam sciéntiam salútis plebi eius: in remissiónem peccatórum eórum;

Through the bowels of the mercy of our God: in which the Orient from on high hath visited us.

To enlighten them that sit in darkness, and in the shadow of death: to direct our feet to the way of peace.

Glory be to the Father and to the Son and to the Holy Ghost.

As it was in the beginning, is now, and ever shall be, world without end. Amen.

Ant. God spared not His own Son, but delivered Him up for all.

℣. Lord, have mercy on us.
℟. Christ, have mercy on us.
℣. Lord, have mercy on us.

Per víscera misericórdiæ Dei nostri: in quibus visitávit nos óriens ex alto.

Illumináre his qui in ténebris et in umbra mortis sedent: ad dirigéndos pedes nostros in viam pacis.

Glória Patri, et Fílio, et Spirítui Sancto.

Sicut erat in princípio, et nunc, et semper, et in sǽcula sæculórum. Amen.

Ant. Próprio Fílio suo non pepércit Deus, sed pro nobis ómnibus trádidit illum.

℣. Kýrie eléison.
℟. Christe eléison.
℣. Kýrie eléison.

Oratio

℣. Let us pray.
O Lord Jesus Christ, at the hour of Matins, Thou chose to be handed over, seized, bound, scourged, buffeted, and spit upon for the salvation of the human race: make us joyfully accept, we beseech Thee, reproaches and injuries for the glory of Thy name, and so keep the memory of this, Thy most holy Passion, ever in mind, that we may happily merit to attain a share of Thy resurrection: Who

℣. Orémus.
Dómine Iesu Christe, qui hora matutína pro salúte humáni géneris tradi, capi, ligári, flagellári, cólaphis cædi et cónspui voluísti: fac nos, quǽsumus, contumélias et oppróbria pro tui nóminis glória lætánter suscípere, et sic huius tuæ sacratíssimæ passiónis memóriam continue recordári; ut ad tuæ resurrectiónis consórtium mereámur felíciter perveníre: Qui vivis et regnas cum Deo Patre in unitáte

live and reign with God the Father in the unity of the Holy Ghost, God, forever and ever.

℟. Amen.

Spíritus Sancti, Deus, per ómnia sǽcula sæculórum.

℟. Amen.

Conclusion

℣. O Lord, hear my prayer.

℟. And let my cry come unto Thee.
℣. Let us bless the Lord.
℟. Thanks be to God.
℣. May the souls of the faithful departed, through the mercy of God, rest in peace.
℟. Amen.

℣. Dómine, exáudi oratiónem meam.
℟. Et clamor meus ad te véniat.
℣. Benedicámus Dómino.
℟. Deo grátias.
℣. Fidélium ánimæ, per misericórdiam Dei, requiéscant in pace.
℟. Amen.

Tu es sanctus Dominus Deus solus, qui facis mirabilia.
Thou art holy, Lord God, who alone works wonders.

The Judging before Pilate
Philadelphia, Free Library of Philadelphia, 1945-65-13, 218.

Prime

℣. O God, ✠ come to my assistance.
℟. O Lord, make haste to help me.
℣. Glory be to the Father, and to the Son, and to the Holy Ghost.
℟. As it was in the beginning, is now, and ever shall be, world without end. Amen. Alleluia.

℣. Deus, ✠ in adiutórium meum inténde.
℟. Dómine, ad adiuvándum me festína.
℣. Glória Patri, et Fílio, et Spirítui Sancto.
℟. Sicut erat in princípio, et nunc, et semper, et in sǽcula sæculórum. Amen. Allelúia.

HYMN

O Sun of Justice, Thou whose rays
By sinful hands were veiled from gaze,
O Thou who, mocked on bended knee,
Was scourged for us most piteously.

With fervent love, O Lord, we pray,
Have mercy on our souls today;
And lead us from this dark world's night
To see in heaven Thy glorious light.

Tu qui velátus fácie
Fuísti, sol iustítiæ,
Flexis illúsus génibus,
Crebris cæsus verbéribus.

Te pétimus atténtius,
Ut sis nobis propítius,
Et per tuam cleméntiam
Perdúcas nos ad glóriam.

To Christ, the Lord of Majesty,
Betrayed and sold to set us free,
Who suffered on the cruel tree,
Be praise and honor endlessly.
Amen.

Ant. I turned not away My face from them that rebuked Me and spat upon Me.

PSALM 42 *Judica me*

JUDGE me, O God, and distinguish my cause from the nation that is not holy: deliver me from the unjust and deceitful man.

For Thou art God my strength: why hast Thou cast me off? And why do I go sorrowful while the enemy afflicteth me?

Send forth Thy light and Thy truth: they have conducted me, and brought me until Thy holy hill, and into Thy tabernacles.

And I will go in to the altar of God: to God who giveth joy to my youth.

To Thee, O God my God, I will give praise upon the harp: why art thou sad, O my soul? And why dost thou disquiet me?

Hope in God, for I will still give praise to him: the salvation of my countenance, and my God.

Laus, honor Christo véndito
Et sine causa pródito,
Mortem passo pro pópulo
In áspero patíbulo. Amen.

Ant. Fáciem meam non avérti ab increpántibus et conspuéntibus in me.

JÚDICA me, Deus, et discérne causam meam de gente non sancta: ab hómine iníquo et dolóso érue me.

Quia tu es, Deus, fortitúdo mea: quare me repulísti? Et quare tristis incédo, dum afflígit me inimícus?

Emítte lucem tuam et veritátem tuam: ipsa me deduxérunt, et adduxérunt in montem sanctum tuum, et in tabernácula tua.

Et introíbo ad altáre Dei: ad Deum qui lætíficat iuventútem meam.

Confitébor tibi in cíthara, Deus, Deus meus: quare tristis es, ánima mea, et quare contúrbas me?

Spera in Deo, quóniam adhuc confitébor illi: salutáre vultus mei, et Deus meus.

Glory be to the Father and to the Son and to the Holy Ghost.

As it was in the beginning, is now, and ever shall be, world without end. Amen.

Ant. I turned not away My face from them that rebuked Me and spat upon Me.

Glória Patri, et Fílio, et Spirítui Sancto.

Sicut erat in princípio, et nunc, et semper, et in sǽcula sæculórum. Amen.

Ant. Fáciem meam non avérti ab increpántibus et conspuéntibus in me.

Capitulum

℣. Think diligently upon Him that endured such opposition from sinners against Himself, that you be not wearied, fainting in your minds.
℟. Thanks be to God.
℣. When He was reviled, He did not revile.
℟. And when He suffered, He threatened not.

℣. Lord, have mercy on us.
℟. Christ, have mercy on us.
℣. Lord, have mercy on us.

℣. Recogitáte eum qui talem sustínuit advérsum semetípsum a peccatóribus contradictiónem, ut non fatigémini ánimis vestris deficiéntes.
℟. Deo grátias.
℣. Cum maledicerétur, non maledicébat.
℟. Et cum paterétur, non comminabátur.

℣. Kýrie eléison.
℟. Christe eléison.
℣. Kýrie eléison.

Oratio

℣. Let us pray.
O Lord Jesus Christ, at the hour of Prime, presented to the governor Pilate for us sinners, Thou the Judge of judges received the harshest sentence: we humbly ask Thee to aid us in our misery when we shall be judged, that in that last judgment we may not be condemned to eter-

℣. Orémus.
Dómine Iesu Christe, qui hora diéi prima pro nobis peccatóribus, Piláto præsidi præsentátus, Iudex iúdicum duríssimum iudícium pertulísti: tibi humíliter supplicámus, ut nobis míseris subvénias iudicándis, ne in extrémo iudício ætérno damnémur supplício, sed tuis in

nal punishment, but may merit to have fellowship with Thy faithful in heaven: Who live and reign with God the Father in the unity of the Holy Ghost, God, forever and ever.

℟. Amen.

cæléstibus mereámur fidélibus sociári: Qui vivis et regnas cum Deo Patre in unitáte Spíritus Sancti, Deus, per ómnia sǽcula sæculórum.

℟. Amen.

Conclusion

℣. O Lord, hear my prayer.

℟. And let my cry come unto Thee.

℣. Let us bless the Lord.

℟. Thanks be to God.

℣. May the souls of the faithful departed, through the mercy of God, rest in peace.

℟. Amen.

℣. Dómine, exáudi oratiónem meam.

℟. Et clamor meus ad te véniat.

℣. Benedicámus Dómino.

℟. Deo grátias.

℣. Fidélium ánimæ, per misericórdiam Dei, requiéscant in pace.

℟. Amen.

Tu es fortis. Tu es magnus. Tu es altissimus.
Thou art strong. Thou art great. Thou art most high.

The Carrying of the Cross
Philadelphia, Free Library of Philadelphia, 1945-65-4 (Collins Hours), fol. 17v.

Terce

℣. O God, ✠ come to my assistance.
℟. O Lord, make haste to help me.
℣. Glory be to the Father, and to the Son, and to the Holy Ghost.
℟. As it was in the beginning, is now, and ever shall be, world without end. Amen. Alleluia.

℣. Deus, ✠ in adiutórium meum inténde.
℟. Dómine, ad adiuvándum me festína.
℣. Glória Patri, et Fílio, et Spirítui Sancto.
℟. Sicut erat in princípio, et nunc, et semper, et in sǽcula sæculórum. Amen. Allelúia.

HYMN

Thou who at this third hour was led
For guilty man Thy Blood to shed,
Bearing the cross they laid on Thee,
The weight of this world's misery.

O fill our hearts with love, and bless
Our life with fruits of holiness,
Until, when strife is o'er, we stand
Before Thee in the heavenly land.

Hora qui ductus tértia
Fuísti ad supplícia,
Christe, feréndo húmeris
Crucem pro nobis míseris.

Fac nos sic te dilígere,
Vitámque sanctam dúcere,
Ut mereámur réquie
Frui cæléstis pátriæ.

To Christ, the Lord of Majesty,
Betrayed and sold to set us free,
Who suffered on the cruel tree,
Be praise and honor endlessly.
  Amen.

Ant. The Lord was led as a sheep to the slaughter and He opened not His mouth.

PSALM 63 *Exaudi, Deus, orationem*

HEAR, O God, my prayer, when I make supplication to thee: deliver my soul from the fear of the enemy.

Thou hast protected me from the assembly of the malignant: from the multitude of the workers of iniquity.

For they have whetted their tongues like a sword: they have bent their bow a bitter thing, to shoot in secret the undefiled.

They will shoot at him on a sudden, and will not fear: they are resolute in wickedness.

They have talked of hiding snares: they have said, who shall see them?

They have searched after iniquities: they have failed in their search.

Man shall come to a deep heart: and God shall be exalted.

The arrows of children are their wounds: and their tongues against them are made weak.

Laus, honor Christo véndito
Et sine causa pródito,
Mortem passo pro pópulo
In áspero patíbulo. Amen.

Ant. Dóminus tanquam ovis ad occisiónem ductus est et non apéruit os suum.

EXÁUDI, Deus, oratiónem meam cum déprecor: a timóre inimíci éripe ánimam meam.

Protexísti me a convéntu malignántium: a multitúdine operántium iniquitátem.

Quia exacuérunt ut gládium linguas suas: intendérunt arcum rem amáram, ut sagíttent in occúltis immaculátum.

Súbito sagittábunt eum, et non timébunt: firmavérunt sibi sermónem nequam.

Narravérunt ut abscónderent láqueos: dixérunt, Quis vidébit eos?

Scrutáti sunt iniquitátes: defecérunt scrutántes scrutínio.

Accédet homo ad cor altum: et exaltábitur Deus.

Sagíttæ parvulórum factæ sunt plagæ eórum: et infirmátæ sunt contra eos linguæ eórum.

All that saw them were troubled: and every man was afraid.	Conturbáti sunt omnes qui vidébant eos: et tímuit omnis homo.
And they declared the works of God: and understood His doings.	Et annuntiavérunt ópera Dei: et facta eius intellexérunt.
The just shall rejoice in the Lord, and shall hope in Him: and all the upright in heart shall be praised.	Lætábitur iustus in Dómino, et sperábit in eo, et laudabúntur omnes recti corde.
Glory be to the Father and to the Son and to the Holy Ghost.	Glória Patri, et Fílio, et Spirítui Sancto.
As it was in the beginning, is now, and ever shall be, world without end. Amen.	Sicut erat in princípio, et nunc, et semper, et in sǽcula sæculórum. Amen.
Ant. The Lord was led as a sheep to the slaughter and He opened not His mouth.	*Ant.* Dóminus tanquam ovis ad occisiónem ductus est et non apéruit os suum.

Capitulum

℣. Christ suffered for us, leaving you an example that you should follow His steps, who did no sin, neither was guile found in his mouth.

℟. Thanks be to God.

℣. He was offered because it was His own will.

℟. And He Himself bore our iniquities.

℣. Lord, have mercy on us.
℟. Christ, have mercy on us.
℣. Lord, have mercy on us.

℣. Christus passus est pro nobis, vobis réliquens exémplum, ut sequámini vestígia eius, qui peccátum non fecit, nec invéntus est dolus in ore eius.

℟. Deo grátias.

℣. Oblátus est, quia ipse vóluit.

℟. Et peccáta nostra ipse portávit.

℣. Kýrie eléison.
℟. Christe eléison.
℣. Kýrie eléison.

Oratio

℣. Let us pray.

O Lord Jesus Christ, Son of the living God, at the hour of Terce, Thou were led to the torment of the cross for the salvation of the whole world: we humbly beg Thee, that by the power of Thy most holy Passion, Thou may blot out all our sins and mercifully lead us to the everlasting glory of Thy beatitude. Who live and reign with God the Father in the unity of the Holy Ghost, God, forever and ever.

℟. Amen.

℣. Orémus.

Dómine Iesu Christe, Fili Dei vivi, qui hora diéi tértia ad crucis torméntum pro mundi salúte ductus es: te supplíciter exorámus, ut per virtútem tuæ sacratíssimæ passiónis ómnia peccáta nostra déleas et ad tuæ beatitúdinis glóriam sempitérnam misericórditer nos perdúcas: Qui vivis et regnas cum Deo Patre in unitáte Spíritus Sancti, Deus, per ómnia sǽcula sæculórum.

℟. Amen.

Conclusion

℣. O Lord, hear my prayer.

℟. And let my cry come unto Thee.

℣. Let us bless the Lord.

℟. Thanks be to God.

℣. May the souls of the faithful departed, through the mercy of God, rest in peace.

℟. Amen.

℣. Dómine, exáudi oratiónem meam.

℟. Et clamor meus ad te véniat.

℣. Benedicámus Dómino.

℟. Deo grátias.

℣. Fidélium ánimæ, per misericórdiam Dei, requiéscant in pace.

℟. Amen.

Tu es rex omnipotens, tu Pater sancte, Rex caeli et terrae.
Thou art the Almighty King,
Thou, holy Father, King of heaven and earth.

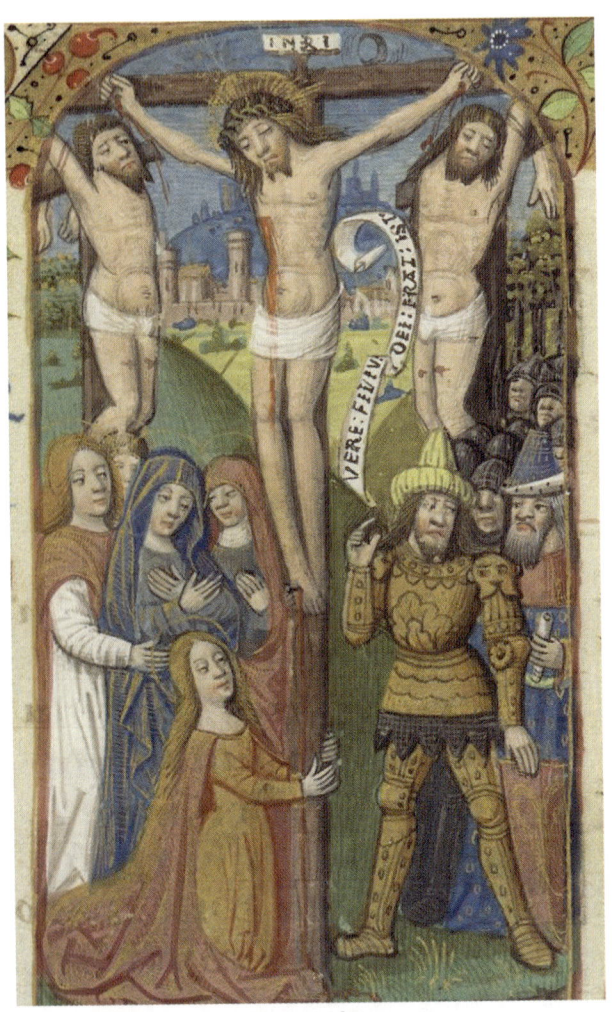

The Crucifixion

Philadelphia, Free Library of Philadelphia, 1945-65-13, p. 227.

Sext

℣. O God, ✠ come to my assistance.
℟. O Lord, make haste to help me.
℣. Glory be to the Father, and to the Son, and to the Holy Ghost.
℟. As it was in the beginning, is now, and ever shall be, world without end. Amen. Alleluia.

℣. Deus, ✠ in adiutórium meum inténde.
℟. Dómine, ad adiuvándum me festína.
℣. Glória Patri, et Fílio, et Spirítui Sancto.
℟. Sicut erat in princípio, et nunc, et semper, et in sǽcula sæculórum. Amen. Allelúia.

HYMN

Jesus was hanged upon the tree
And thirsted in His agony,
In hands and feet He deigned to bear
The cruel nails that held Him there.

Honor and blessing ever be,
O Jesus crucified, to Thee,
Who by Thy death and bitter pain,
Didst bring us exiles home again.

To Christ, the Lord of Majesty,
Betrayed and sold to set us free,
Who suffered on the cruel tree,
Be praise and honor endlessly. Amen.

Crucem pro nobis súbiit,
Et stans in illa sítiit
Iesus, sacrátis mánibus
Clavis fossus et pédibus.

Honor et benedíctio
Sit crucifíxo Fílio,
Qui suo nos supplício
Redémit ab exsílio.

Laus, honor Christo véndito
Et sine causa pródito,
Mortem passo pro pópulo
In áspero patíbulo. Amen.

Ant. They put over His head His cause written, Jesus of Nazareth, King of the Jews.

Ant. Posuérunt super caput eius causam ipsíus scriptam: Iesus Nazarénus, Rex Iudæórum.

PSALM 115 *Credidi*

I HAVE believed, therefore I have spoken: but I have been humbled exceedingly.

I said in my excess: every man is a liar.

What shall I render to the Lord: for all the things that He hath rendered to me?

I will take the chalice of salvation: and I will call upon the name of the Lord.

I will pay my vows to the Lord before all His people: precious in the sight of the Lord is the death of His saints.

O Lord, for I am thy servant: I am thy servant, and the son of Thy handmaid.

Thou hast broken my bonds: I will sacrifice to Thee the sacrifice of praise, and I will call upon the name of the Lord.

I will pay my vows to the Lord in the sight of all his people: in the courts of the house of the Lord, in the midst of Thee, O Jerusalem.

Glory be to the Father and to the Son and to the Holy Ghost.

As it was in the beginning, is now, and ever shall be, world without end. Amen.

CRÉDIDI, propter quod locútus sum: ego autem humiliátus sum nimis.

Ego dixi in excéssu meo: omnis homo mendax.

Quid retríbuam Dómino: pro ómnibus quæ retríbuit mihi?

Cálicem salutáris accípiam: et nomen Dómini invocábo.

Vota mea Dómino reddam coram omni pópulo eius: pretiósa in conspéctu Dómini mors sanctórum eius.

O Dómine, quia ego servus tuus: ego servus tuus, et fílius ancíllæ tuæ.

Dirupísti víncula mea: tibi sacrificábo hóstiam laudis, et nomen Dómini invocábo.

Vota mea Dómino reddam in conspéctu omnis pópuli eius: in átriis domus Dómini, in médio tui, Ierúsalem.

Glória Patri, et Fílio, et Spirítui Sancto.

Sicut erat in princípio, et nunc, et semper, et in sæcula sæculórum. Amen.

Ant. They put over His head His cause written, Jesus of Nazareth, King of the Jews.

Ant. Posuérunt super caput eius causam ipsíus scriptam: Iesus Nazarénus, Rex Iudæórum.

Capitulum

℣. He delivered himself to him that judged Him unjustly, He who bore our sins in His body on the tree, that we, being dead to sins, should live to justice: by whose stripes we were healed.
℟. Thanks be to God.
℣. He was offered because it was His own will.
℟. And He Himself bore our iniquities.

℣. Lord, have mercy on us.
℟. Christ, have mercy on us.
℣. Lord, have mercy on us.

℣. Tradébat autem iudicánti se iniúste, qui peccáta nostra ipse pértulit in córpore suo super lignum, ut peccátis mórtui iustítiæ vivámus, cuius livóre sanáti sumus.
℟. Deo grátias.
℣. Oblátus est, quia ipse vóluit.
℟. Et peccáta nostra ipse portávit.

℣. Kýrie eléison.
℟. Christe eléison.
℣. Kýrie eléison.

Oratio

℣. Let us pray.
O Lord Jesus Christ, at the hour of Sext, Thou climbed the gibbet of the cross and, thirsting for our salvation, Thou allowed Thyself to drink gall and vinegar: we humbly beg Thee, with our hearts enkindled and inflamed, to make us thirst for the chalice of Thy passion: Who live and reign with God the Father in the unity of the Holy Ghost, God, forever and ever.
℟. Amen.

℣. Orémus.
Dómine Iesu Christe, qui hora diéi sexta crucis patíbulum ascendísti, in qua, salútem nostram sítiens, felle et acéto te potáre permisísti: te supplíciter deprecámur; ut accénso et inflammáto corde nostro sitíre nos fácias tuæ cálicem passiónis: Qui vivis et regnas cum Deo Patre in unitáte Spíritus Sancti, Deus, per ómnia sǽcula sæculórum.
℟. Amen.

Conclusion

℣. O Lord, hear my prayer.

℟. And let my cry come unto Thee.

℣. Let us bless the Lord.

℟. Thanks be to God.

℣. May the souls of the faithful departed, through the mercy of God, rest in peace.

℟. Amen.

℣. Dómine, exáudi oratiónem meam.

℟. Et clamor meus ad te véniat.

℣. Benedicámus Dómino.

℟. Deo grátias.

℣. Fidélium ánimæ, per misericórdiam Dei, requiéscant in pace.

℟. Amen.

Tu es trinus et unus Dominus Deus, omne bonum.
Thou art the Lord God Triune and One, all good.

The Deposition
Philadelphia, Free Library of Philadelphia, 1945-65-13, p. 230.

None

℣. O God, ✠ come to my assistance.
℟. O Lord, make haste to help me.
℣. Glory be to the Father, and to the Son, and to the Holy Ghost.
℟. As it was in the beginning, is now, and ever shall be, world without end. Amen. Alleluia.

℣. Deus, ✠ in adiutórium meum inténde.
℟. Dómine, ad adiuvándum me festína.
℣. Glória Patri, et Fílio, et Spirítui Sancto.
℟. Sicut erat in princípio, et nunc, et semper, et in sǽcula sæculórum. Amen. Allelúia.

HYMN

May Christ's most blessed Passion win
Deliverance from death and sin,
Whereby to man the hope is given
Of everlasting joys in heaven.

Glory to Christ our Lord on high
Who, with one last triumphant cry,
Gave up His soul upon the cross
And saved the world from endless loss.

To Christ, the Lord of Majesty,
Betrayed and sold to set us free
Who suffered on the cruel tree,
Be praise and honor endlessly. Amen.

Beáta Christi póssio
Sit nostra liberátio,
Ut per hanc nobis gáudia
Paráta sint cæléstia.

Glória Christo Dómino,
Qui pendens in patíbulo,
Clamans emísit spíritum,
Mundúmque salvans pérditum.

Laus, honor Christo véndito
Et sine causa pródito,
Mortem passo pro pópulo
In áspero patíbulo. Amen.

Ant. When Jesus had taken the vinegar, He said: It is consummated. And bowing His head, He gave up the ghost.

Ant. Cum accepísset Iesus acétum, dixit: Consummátum est. Et inclináto cápite, emísit spíritum.

PSALM 141 *Voce mea*

I CRIED to the Lord with my voice: with my voice I made supplication to the Lord.

In His sight I pour out my prayer: and before him I declare my trouble.

When my spirit failed me: then Thou knewest my paths.

In this way wherein I walked: they have hidden a snare for me.

I looked on my right hand, and beheld: and there was no one that would know me.

Flight hath failed me: and there is no one that hath regard to my soul.

I cried to thee, O Lord, I said: Thou art my hope, my portion in the land of the living.

Attend to my supplication: for I am brought very low.

Deliver me from my persecutors: for they are stronger than I.

Bring my soul out of prison, that I may praise Thy name: the just wait for me, until Thou reward me.

VOCE mea ad Dóminum clamávi: voce mea ad Dóminum deprecátus sum.

Effúndo in conspéctu eius oratiónem meam: et tribulatiónem meam ante ipsum pronúntio.

In deficiéndo ex me spíritum meum: et tu cognovísti sémitas meas.

In via hac qua ambulábam: abscondérunt láqueum mihi.

Considerábam ad déxteram, et vidébam: et non erat qui cognósceret me.

Périit fuga a me: et non est qui requírat ánimam meam.

Clamávi ad te, Dómine, dixi: Tu es spes mea, pórtio mea in terra vivéntium.

Inténde ad deprecatiónem meam: quia humiliátus sum nimis.

Líbera me a persequéntibus me: quia confortáti sunt super me.

Educ de custódia ánimam meam ad confiténdum nómini tuo: me exspéctant iusti, donec retríbuas mihi.

Glory be to the Father and to the Son and to the Holy Ghost.

As it was in the beginning, is now, and ever shall be, world without end. Amen.

Ant. When Jesus had taken the vinegar, He said: It is consummated. And bowing His head, He gave up the ghost.

Glória Patri, et Fílio, et Spirítui Sancto.

Sicut erat in princípio, et nunc, et semper, et in sǽcula sæculórum. Amen.

Ant. Cum accepísset Iesus acétum, dixit: Consummátum est. Et inclináto cápite, emísit spíritum.

Capitulum

℣. It became Him for whom are all things and by whom are all things, who had brought many children into glory, to perfect the author of their salvation by His Passion.

℟. Thanks be to God.

℣. He delivered His soul unto death.

℟. And He was reputed with the wicked.

℣. Lord, have mercy on us.
℟. Christ, have mercy on us.
℣. Lord, have mercy on us.

℣. Decébat eum, per quem ómnia et propter quem ómnia facta sunt, qui multos fílios in glóriam addúxerat, auctórem salútis eórum per passiónem consummári.

℟. Deo grátias.

℣. Trádidit in mortem ánimam suam.

℟. Et cum viris scelerátis deputátus est.

℣. Kýrie eléison.
℟. Christe eléison.
℣. Kýrie eléison.

Oratio

℣. Let us pray.

O Lord Jesus Christ, at the hour of None, with arms outstretched on the cross and head bowed down, Thou handed over the spirit to God the Father and Thou most worthily unlocked paradise with the key of Thy death: grant to us, who though

℣. Orémus.

Dómine Iesu Christe, qui hora diéi nona, expánsis in cruce mánibus et inclináto cápite, Deo Patri spíritum tradidísti et clave mortis tuæ dignantíssime paradísum reserásti: concéde nobis indígnis supplícibus tuis; ut in hora mortis nostræ ánimas

unworthy, come before Thee in humble prayer, that in the hour of our death Thou may mercifully make our souls attain Thee, who are the true paradise: Who live and reign with God the Father in the unity of the Holy Ghost, God, forever and ever.

℟. Amen.

nostras ad te, qui verus paradísus es, fácias misericórditer veníre: Qui vivis et regnas cum Deo Patre in unitáte Spíritus Sancti, Deus, per ómnia sǽcula sæculórum.

℟. Amen.

Conclusion

℣. O Lord, hear my prayer.

℟. And let my cry come unto Thee.

℣. Let us bless the Lord.

℟. Thanks be to God.

℣. May the souls of the faithful departed, through the mercy of God, rest in peace.

℟. Amen.

℣. Dómine, exáudi oratiónem meam.

℟. Et clamor meus ad te véniat.

℣. Benedicámus Dómino.

℟. Deo grátias.

℣. Fidélium ánimæ, per misericórdiam Dei, requiéscant in pace.

℟. Amen.

Tu es bonum, omne bonum, summum bonum,
Dominus Deus, vivus et verus.
Thou art good, all good, highest good,
Lord God living and true.

The Harrowing of Hell
Philadelphia, Free Library of Philadelphia, 1945-65-4 (Collins Hours), fol. 24v.

Vespers

℣. O God, ✠ come to my assistance.
℟. O Lord, make haste to help me.
℣. Glory be to the Father, and to the Son, and to the Holy Ghost.
℟. As it was in the beginning, is now, and ever shall be, world without end. Amen. Alleluia.

Ant. Thou art worthy, O Lord, to take the book and to open the seven seals thereof, because Thou were slain and have redeemed us to God in Thy blood.

℣. Deus, ✠ in adiutórium meum inténde.
℟. Dómine, ad adiuvándum me festína.
℣. Glória Patri, et Fílio, et Spirítui Sancto.
℟. Sicut erat in princípio, et nunc, et semper, et in sǽcula sæculórum. Amen. Allelúia.

Ant. Dignus es, Dómine, accípere librum et aperíre septem signácula eius, quóniam occísus es et redemísti nos Deo in sánguine tuo.

PSALM 29 *Exaltabo te, Domine*

I WILL extol Thee, O Lord, for Thou hast upheld me: and hast not made my enemies to rejoice over me.

O Lord my God, I have cried to Thee: and Thou hast healed me.

Thou hast brought forth, O Lord, my soul from hell: Thou hast saved me from them that go down into the pit.

EXALTÁBO te, Dómine, quóniam suscepísti me: nec delectásti inimícos meos super me.

Dómine Deus meus, clamávi ad te: et sanásti me.

Dómine, eduxísti ab inférno ánimam meam: salvásti me a descendéntibus in lacum.

Sing to the Lord, O ye His saints: and give praise to the memory of His holiness.	Psállite Dómino, sancti eius: et confitémini memóriæ sanctitátis eius.
For wrath is in His indignation: and life in His good will.	Quóniam ira in indignatióne eius: et vita in voluntáte eius.
In the evening weeping shall have place: and in the morning gladness.	Ad vésperum demorábitur fletus: et ad matutínum lætítia.
And in my abundance I said: I shall never be moved.	Ego autem dixi in abundántia mea: Non movébor in ætérnum.
O Lord, in thy favor: thou gavest strength to my beauty.	Dómine, in voluntáte tua: præstitísti decóri meo virtútem.
Thou turnedst away Thy face from me: and I became troubled.	Avertísti fáciem tuam a me: et factus sum conturbátus.
To Thee, O Lord, will I cry: and I will make supplication to my God.	Ad te, Dómine, clamábo: et ad Deum meum deprecábor.
What profit is there in my blood: whilst I go down to corruption?	Quæ utílitas in sánguine meo: dum descéndo in corruptiónem?
Shall dust confess to Thee: or declare Thy truth?	Numquid confitébitur tibi pulvis: aut annuntiábit veritátem tuam?
The Lord hath heard, and hath had mercy on me: the Lord became my helper.	Audívit Dóminus, et misértus est mei: Dóminus factus est adiútor meus.
Thou hast turned for me my mourning into joy: Thou hast cut my sackcloth, and hast compassed me with gladness:	Convertísti planctum meum in gáudium mihi: conscidísti saccum meum, et circumdedísti me lætítia:
To the end that my glory may sing to Thee, and I may not regret: O Lord my God, I will give praise to Thee forever.	Ut cantet tibi glória mea, et non compúngar: Dómine Deus meus, in ætérnum confitébor tibi.

Glory be to the Father and to the Son and to the Holy Ghost.

As it was in the beginning, is now, and ever shall be, world without end. Amen.

Ant. Thou art worthy, O Lord, to take the book and to open the seven seals thereof, because Thou were slain and have redeemed us to God in Thy blood.

Glória Patri, et Fílio, et Spirítui Sancto.

Sicut erat in princípio, et nunc, et semper, et in sǽcula sæculórum. Amen.

Ant. Dignus es, Dómine, accípere librum et aperíre septem signácula eius, occísus es et redemísti nos Deo in sánguine tuo.

Capitulum

℣. We see Jesus crowned with glory and honor for suffering death; that, through the grace of God, He might taste death for all.

℟. Thanks be to God.

℣. Vidémus Iesum propter passiónem mortis glória et honóre coronátum, ut grátia Dei pro ómnibus gustáret mortem.

℟. Deo grátias.

HYMN

O Thou who through death's agony
For man didst break sin's barrier down
Bring us to find true peace in Thee,
Jesus, who art the Virgin's crown.

A bitter potion Thou didst drain
'Mid cruel scorn and suffering
Thou spotless Lamb for sinners slain,
O Lord Most High, eternal King.

Qui pressúra mortis dura
Solvísti nexus críminum,
Nos ad pacem duc verácem,
Iesu, coróna vírginum.

In flagéllis potum fellis
Bibísti amaríssime
Pro peccátis perpetrátis,
ætérne Rex altíssime.

To all Thy faithful, who this day Thy sacred Passion bear in mind, Give saving health and grace to pray, Jesus, Redeemer of mankind.	Omni genti recolénti Tuæ mortis supplícium Da virtútem et salútem, Iesu redémptor ómnium.
Upon the altar of the tree Flowed forth in streams Thy Blood divine, O Jesus, King of clemency, In whom the Father's light doth shine.	In amára crucis ara Fudísti rivos sánguinis, Iesu digne, Rex benígne, Consors patérni lúminis.
O Blood of Christ, whose glorious might Did strike the demon with despair, Grant we may come in robes of white The Lamb's great marriage feast to share.	Sanguis Christi, qui fuísti Perémptor hostis invídi. Fac secúre nos veníre Ad cœnam Agni próvidi.
To Christ, the Lord of Majesty, Betrayed and sold to set us free, Who suffered on the cruel tree, Be praise and honor endlessly. Amen.	Laus, honor Christo véndito Et sine causa pródito, Mortem passo pro pópulo In áspero patíbulo. Amen.

℣. The chastisement of our sins was upon Him.
℟. For by His stripes we are healed.

℣. Disciplína pacis nostræ super eum.
℟. Quia livóre eius sanáti sumus.

Ant. Our Shepherd, the fountain of living water, is gone, for He laid down his life for His sheep and vouchsafed to die for His flock.

Ant. Recéssit pastor noster bonus, fons aquæ vivæ, quia ánimam suam pósuit pro óvibus suis et pro suo grege mori dignátus est.

THE MAGNIFICAT *Lk.* 1:46-55

MY soul ✠ doth magnify the Lord.

And my spirit hath rejoiced: in God my savior.

Because he hath regarded the humility of His handmaid: for behold from henceforth all generations will call me blessed.

Because He that is mighty, hath done great things to me: and holy his His name.

And His mercy is from generation unto generations: to them that fear Him.

He hath shown might in His arm: He hath scattered the proud in the conceit of their heart.

He hath put down the mighty from their seat: and hath exalted the humble.

He hath filled the hungry with good things: and the rich He hath sent empty away.

He hath received Israel his servant: being mindful of his mercy,

As He spoke to our fathers: to Abraham and to his seed forever.

Glory be to the Father and to the Son and to the Holy Ghost.

As it was in the beginning, is now, and ever shall be, world without end. Amen.

MAGNÍFICAT ✠ ánima mea Dóminum.

Et exsultávit Spíritus meus: in Deo salutári meo.

Quia respéxit humilitátem ancíllæ suæ: ecce enim ex hoc beátam me dicent omnes generatiónes.

Quia fecit mihi magna qui potens est: et sanctum nomen eius.

Et misericórdia eius a progénie in progénies: timéntibus eum.

Fecit poténtiam in bráchio suo: dispérsit supérbos mente cordis sui.

Depósuit poténtes de sede: et exaltávit húmiles.

Esuriéntes implévit bonis: et dívites dimísit ináes.

Suscépit Israël púerum suum: recordátus misericórdiæ suæ,

Sicut locútus est ad patres nostros: Ábraham et sémini eius in sæcula.

Glória Patri, et Fílio, et Spirítui Sancto.

Sicut erat in princípio, et nunc, et semper, et in sǽcula sæculórum. Amen.

Ant. Our Shepherd, the fountain of living water, is gone, for He laid down his life for His sheep and vouchsafed to die for His flock.

℣. Lord, have mercy on us.
℟. Christ, have mercy on us.
℣. Lord, have mercy on us.

Ant. Recéssit pastor noster bonus, fons aquæ vivæ, quia ánimam suam pósuit pro óvibus suis et pro suo grege mori dignátus est.

℣. Kýrie eléison.
℟. Christe eléison.
℣. Kýrie eléison.

Oratio

℣. Let us pray.
O Lord Jesus Christ, at the hour of Vespers, for the salvation of the human race, already taken away by death, Thou chose to be taken down from the cross and laid in the hands of Thy Mother, as is piously believed: kindly grant, with the burden of our sins laid aside, we may be presented before the sight of Thy divine Majesty: Who live and reign with God the Father in the unity of the Holy Ghost, God, forever and ever.
℟. Amen.

℣. Orémus.
Dómine Iesu Christe, qui hora vespertína, pro humána salúte iam morte perémptus, de cruce depóni et in tuæ Matris mánibus, ut pie créditur, récipi voluísti: concéde propítius; ut depósitis peccatórum nostrórum sarcínis, ante conspéctum divínæ Maiestátis tuæ præsentári valeámus: Qui vivis et regnas cum Deo Patre in unitáte Spíritus Sancti, Deus, per ómnia sǽcula sæculórum.
℟. Amen.

Conclusion

℣. O Lord, hear my prayer.
℟. And let my cry come unto thee.
℣. Let us bless the Lord.
℟. Thanks be to God.

℣. Dómine, exáudi oratiónem meam.
℟. Et clamor meus ad te véniat.
℣. Benedicámus Dómino.
℟. Deo grátias.

℣. May the souls of the faithful departed, through the mercy of God, rest in peace.
℟. Amen.

℣. Fidélium ánimæ, per misericórdiam Dei, requiéscant in pace.
℟. Amen.

Tu es caritas, amor. Tu es sapientia. Tu es humilitas.
Thou art charity, love. Thou art wisdom. Thou art humility.

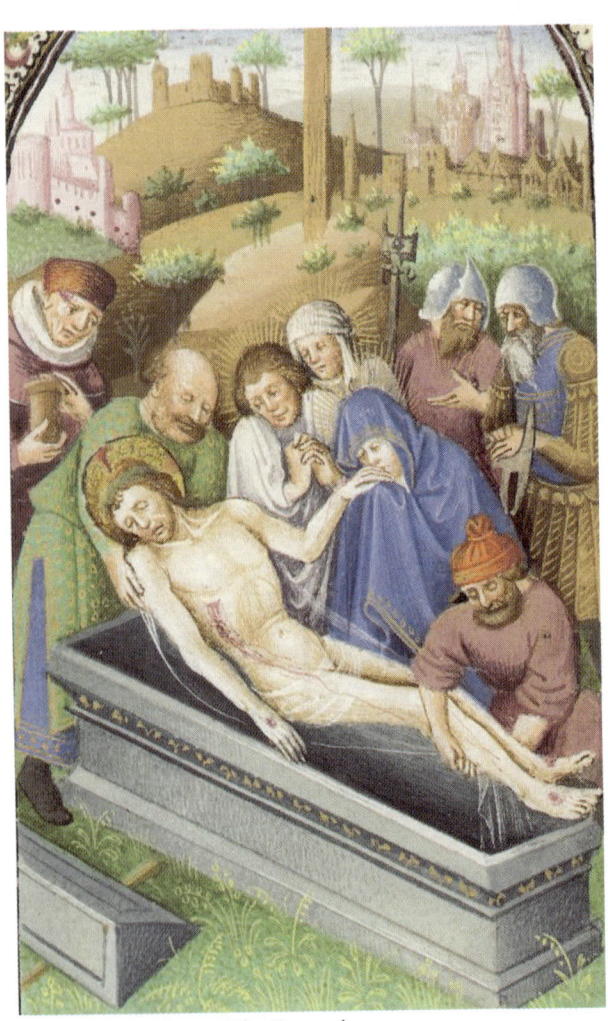

The Entombment
Philadelphia, Free Library of Philadelphia, 1945-65-4 (Collins Hours), fol. 20v.

Compline

℣. Convert us, O God our Savior.

℟. And turn away thine anger from us.

℣. O God, ✠ come to my assistance.

℟. O Lord, make haste to help me.

℣. Glory be to the Father, and to the Son, and to the Holy Ghost.

℟. As it was in the beginning, is now, and ever shall be, world without end. Amen. Alleluia.

Ant. They shall mourn for Him as for an only son, because the innocent Lord is slain.

℣. Convérte nos, Deus salutáris noster.

℟. Et avérte iram tuam a nobis.

℣. Deus, ✠ in adiutórium meum inténde.

℟. Dómine, ad adiuvándum me festína.

℣. Glória Patri, et Fílio, et Spirítui Sancto.

℟. Sicut erat in princípio, et nunc, et semper, et in sǽcula sæculórum. Allelúia.

Ant. Plangent eum quasi unigénitum, quia ínnocens Dóminus occísus est.

PSALM 87 *Domine, Deus salutis*

O LORD, the God of my salvation: I have cried in the day, and in the night before Thee.

Let my prayer come in before Thee: incline Thy ear to my petition.

For my soul is filled with evils: and my life hath drawn nigh to hell.

DÓMINE, Deus salútis meæ: in die clamávi et nocte coram te.

Intret in conspéctu tuo orátio mea: inclína aurem tuam ad precem meam.

Quia repléta est malis ánima mea: et vita mea inférno appropinquávit.

I am counted among them that go down into the pit: I am become as a man without help, free among the dead.

Like the slain sleeping in the sepulchres, whom Thou rememberest no more: and they are cast off from Thy hand.

They have laid me in the lower pit: in the dark places, and in the shadow of death.

Thy wrath is strong over me: and all Thy waves Thou hast brought in upon me.

Thou hast put away my acquaintance far from me: they have set me an abomination to themselves.

I was delivered up, and came not forth: my eyes languished through poverty.

All the day I cried to Thee, O Lord: I stretched out my hands to thee.

Wilt thou show wonders to the dead: or shall physicians raise to life, and give praise to Thee?

Shall anyone in the sepulchre declare Thy mercy: and Thy truth in destruction?

Shall Thy wonders be known in the dark: and Thy justice in the hand of forgetfulness?

But I, O Lord, have cried to Thee: and in the morning my prayer shall prevent Thee.

Æstimátus sum cum descendéntibus in lacum: factus sum sicut homo sine adiutório, inter mórtuos liber.

Sicut vulneráti dormiéntes in sepúlchris, quorum non es memor ámplius: et ipsi de manu tua repúlsi sunt.

Posuérunt me in lacu inferióri: in tenebrósis, et in umbra mortis.

Super me confirmátus est furor tuus: et omnes fluctus tuos induxísti super me.

Longe fecísti notos meos a me: posuérunt me abominatiónem sibi.

Tráditus sum, et non egrediébar: óculi mei languérunt præ inópia.

Clamávi ad te, Dómine, tota die: expándi ad te manus meas.

Numquid mórtuis fácies mirabília: aut médici suscitábunt, et confitebúntur tibi?

Numquid narrábit áliquis in sepúlchro misericórdiam tuam: et veritátem tuam in perditióne?

Numquid cognoscéntur in ténebris mirabília tua: et iustítia tua in terra obliviónis?

Et ego ad te, Dómine, clamávi: et mane orátio mea prævéniet te.

Lord, why castest Thou off my prayer: why turnest Thou away Thy face from me?

I am poor, and in labors from my youth: and being exalted have been humbled and troubled.

Thy wrath has come upon me: and Thy terrors have troubled me.

They have come round about me like water all the day: they have compassed me about together.

Friend and neighbor Thou hast put far from me: and my acquaintance, because of misery.

Glory be to the Father and to the Son and to the Holy Ghost.

As it was in the beginning, is now, and ever shall be, world without end. Amen.

Ant. They shall mourn for Him as for an only son, because the innocent Lord is slain.

Ut quid, Dómine, repéllis oratiónem meam: avértis fáciem tuam a me?

Pauper sum ego, et in labóribus a iuventúte mea: exaltátus autem, humiliátus sum et conturbátus.

In me transiérunt iræ tuæ: et terróres tui conturbavérunt me.

Circumdedérunt me sicut aqua tota die: circumdedérunt me simul.

Elongásti a me amícum et próximum: et notos meos a miséria.

Glória Patri, et Fílio, et Spirítui Sancto.

Sicut erat in princípio, et nunc, et semper, et in sæcula sæculórum. Amen.

Ant. Plangent eum quasi unigénitum, quia ínnocens Dóminus occísus est.

HYMN

O sinless King, who at the close
Of day didst in the rock repose,
Do Thou our restless passions still
And win our hearts to do Thy will.

Qui iacuísti mórtuus
In petra rex innócuus,
Fac nos in te quiéscere,
Sanctámque vitam dúcere.

Lord, succor in the conflict dread The soul for whom Thy Blood was shed, And bring us when life's trials cease To rest in Thine eternal peace.	Succúrre nobis, Dómine Quos redemísti sánguine, Et duc nos ad cæléstia ætérnæ pacis gáudia.
To Christ, the Lord of Majesty, Betrayed and sold to set us free, Who suffered on the cruel tree, Be praise and honor endlessly. Amen.	Laus, honor Christo véndito Et sine causa pródito, Mortem passo pro pópulo In áspero patíbulo. Amen

Capitulum

℣. Christ having suffered in the flesh, be you also armed with the same thought.
℟. Thanks be to God.
℣. And His place is in peace.

℟. And His abode in Sion.

Ant. Savior of the world, save us: Thou who didst redeem us by thy Cross and Blood, aid us, we beseech thee, O Lord our God.

℣. Christo in carne passo, et vos eádem cogitatióne armámini.
℟. Deo grátias.
℣. Et factus est in pace locus eius.
℟. Et habitátio eius in Sion.

Ant. Salvátor mundi, salva nos, qui per crucem et sánguinem redemísti nos, auxiliáre nobis, te deprecámur, Deus noster.

CANTICLE OF SIMEON *Lk.* 2:29-32

NOW Thou dost dismiss Thy servant, O Lord: according to Thy word in peace.

Because my eyes have seen: Thy salvation,

Which Thou hast prepared: before the face of all peoples,

NUNC dimíttis servum tuum, Dómine: secúndum verbum tuum in pace.

Quia vidérunt óculi mei: salutáre tuum,

Quod parásti: ante fáciem ómnium populórum.

A light to the revelation of the Gentiles: and the glory of Thy people Israel.

Glory be to the Father and to the Son and to the Holy Ghost.

As it was in the beginning, is now, and ever shall be, world without end. Amen.

Ant. Savior of the world, save us: Thou who didst redeem us by thy Cross and Blood, aid us, we beseech thee, O Lord our God.

℣. Lord, have mercy on us.
℟. Christ, have mercy on us.
℣. Lord, have mercy on us.
Our Father *(in secret until)*
℣. And lead us not into temptation.
℟. But deliver us from evil.

Lumen ad revelatiónem géntium: et glóriam plebis tuæ Israël.

Glória Patri, et Fílio, et Spirítui Sancto.

Sicut erat in princípio, et nunc, et semper, et in sǽcula sæculórum. Amen.

Ant. Salvátor mundi, salva nos, qui per crucem et sánguinem redemísti nos, auxiliáre nobis, te deprecámur, Deus noster.

℣. Kýrie eléison.
℟. Christe eléison.
℣. Kýrie eléison.
Pater noster *(secreto usque ad)*
℣. Et ne nos indúcas in tentatiónem.
℟. Sed líbera nos a malo.

Oratio

℣. Let us pray.
O Lord Jesus Christ, at the last hour of the day, Thou rested in the tomb, and were grieved and mourned over by Thy most sorrowful Mother and the other women; make us, we beg, to overflow with tears of compunction for Thy passion, and to mourn it especially at all times, with the full devotion of our hearts, and to keep it as though it were before us through burn-

℣. Orémus.
Dómine Iesu Christe, qui hora diéi última in sepúlcro quievísti, et a Matre tua mœstíssima et ab áliis muliéribus planctus et lamentátus fuísti: fac nos, quǽsumus, passiónis tuæ compunctióne lácrymis abundáre et tota cordis devotióne ipsam passiónem tuam semper plángere eámque quasi recéntem in ardénti desidério retínere: Qui vivis et regnas cum Deo Patre

ing desire: Who live and reign with God the Father in the unity of the Holy Spirit, God, forever and ever.

℟. Amen.

in unitáte Spíritus Sancti, Deus, per ómnia sǽcula sæculórum.

℟. Amen.

Conclusion

℣. O Lord, hear my prayer.

℟. And let my cry come unto Thee.
℣. Let us bless the Lord.
℟. Thanks be to God.
℣. May the almighty and merciful Lord, Father, and Son, and Holy Ghost, bless and preserve us.
℟. Amen.

℣. Dómine, exáudi oratiónem meam.

℟. Et clamor meus ad te véniat.
℣. Benedicámus Dómino.
℟. Deo grátias.
℣. Benedícat et custódiat nos omnípotens et miséricors Dóminus, Pater, et Fílius, et Spíritus Sanctus.
℟. Amen.

Then is said one of the antiphons of the Blessed Virgin, according to the season, after which is said the following:

℣. May the divine assistance remain always with us.
℟. Amen.

℣. Divínum auxílium máneat semper nobíscum.
℟. Amen.

Tu es patientia. Tu es securitas. Tu es quietas.
Thou art patience. Thou art security. Thou art rest.

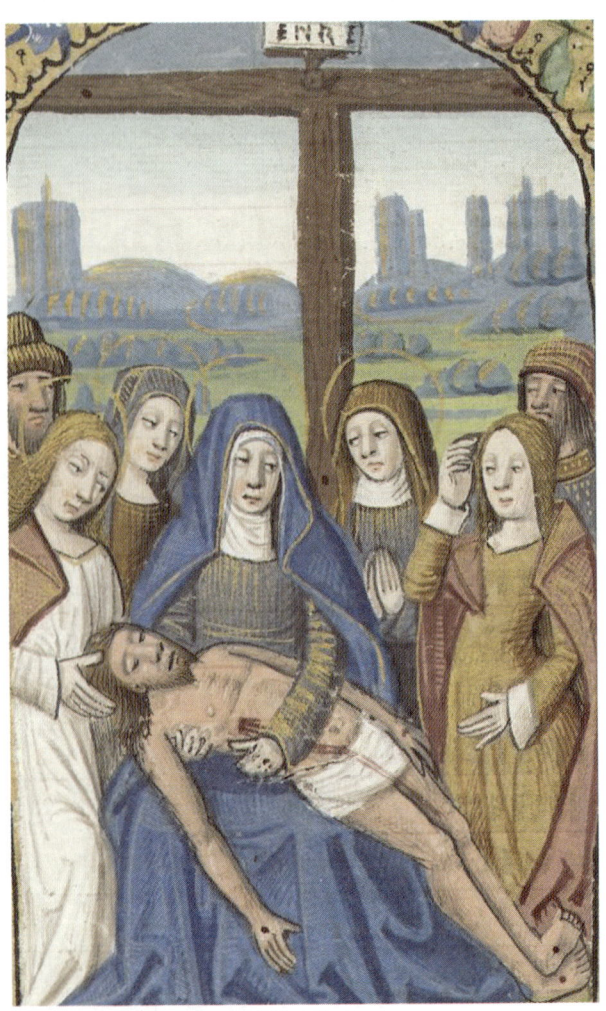

The Pietà

Philadelphia, Free Library of Philadelphia, 1945-65-13, p. 48.

Antiphons of the Blessed Virgin

I

From Vespers of Saturday before the First Sunday of Advent to Second Vespers of the Purification: Solemn Tone, p. 74; Simple Tone, p. 75.

ANTIPHON

LOVING mother of the Redeemer, open door to heaven and star of the sea, come quickly to the aid of thy people, fallen indeed but striving to stand again. To nature's astonishment thou wert the mother of thy holy Creator without ceasing to be a virgin, and heard from Gabriel that greeting: "Hail." Have pity on us sinners.

ALMA Redemptóris Mater, quæ pérvia cæli Porta manes, et stella maris, succúrre cadénti, Súrgere qui curat, pópulo: tu quæ genuísti, Natúra miránte, tuum sanctum Genitórem, Virgo prius ac postérius, Gabriélis ab ore Sumens illud "Ave," peccatórum miserére.

Before December 24

℣. The Angel of the Lord declared unto Mary.

℟. And she conceived by the Holy Ghost.

℣. Angelus Dómini nuntiávit Maríæ.

℟. Et concépit de Spíritu Sancto.

Collect

Let us pray. Pour forth, we beseech Thee, O Lord, Thy grace into our hearts, that we to whom the incarnation of Christ Thy Son was made known by the message of an angel may, by His

Orémus. Grátiam tuam, quáesumus, Dómine, méntibus nostris infúnde: ut qui, Angelo nuntiánte, Christi Fílii tui incarnatiónem cognóvimus; per passiónem ejus et crucem, ad

Passion and Cross, be brought to the glory of His resurrection. Through the same Christ our Lord. ℟. Amen.

resurrectiónis glóriam perducámur. Per eúndem Christum Dóminum.

℟. Amen.

From December 24

℣. Even after giving birth, thou remained a Virgin.

℟. Mother of God, intercede for us.

℣. Post partum, Virgo, inviolata permansísti.

℟. Dei Génetrix, intercéde pro nobis.

Collect

Let us pray. O God, who, by the fruitful virginity of Blessed Mary, hast given to mankind the rewards of eternal salvation; grant, we beseech Thee, that we may experience her intercession for us, through whom we have deserved to receive the Author of life, our Lord Jesus Christ, Thy Son. ℟. Amen.

Orémus. Deus, qui salútis ætérnæ beátæ Maríæ virginitáte fecúnda, humáno géneri præmia præstitísti: tríbue, quǽsumus; ut ipsam pro nobis intercédere sentiámus, per quam merúimus auctórem vitæ suscípere, Dóminum nostrum Jesum Christum, Fílium tuum.

℟. Amen.

II

From Compline of February 2 (even if the Feast of the Purification be transferred) until Compline of Wednesday in Holy Week: Solemn Tone, p. 76; Simple Tone, p. 77.

ANTIPHON

HAIL, Queen of Heaven; hail, Mistress of the Angels; hail, root of Jesse; hail, the gate through which the Light rose over the earth.

Rejoice, Virgin most renowned and of unsurpassed

AVE, Regína cælórum,
Ave, Dómina Angelórum:
Salve, radix, salve, porta,
Ex qua mundo lux est orta:

Gaude, Virgo gloriósa,
Super omnes speciósa,

beauty. Farewell, Lady most comely. Prevail upon Christ to pity us.

℣. Let me praise thee, most holy Virgin.
℟. Give me strength against thine enemies.

Vale, o valde decóra,
Et pro nobis Christum exóra.

℣. Dignáre me laudáre te, Virgo sacráta.
℟. Da mihi virtútem contra hostes tuos.

Collect

Let us pray. Grant, O merciful God, defense to our weakness; that we who now celebrate the memory of the holy Mother of God may, by the aid of her intercession, rise again from our sins. Through the same Christ our Lord. ℟. Amen.

Orémus. Concéde, miséricors Deus, fragilitáti nostræ præsídium: ut, qui sanctæ Dei Genetrícis memóriam ágimus; intercessiónis ejus auxílio, a nostris iniquitátibus resurgámus. Per eúndem Christum Dóminum nostrum. ℟. Amen.

III

From Compline of Easter Sunday to Compline of Friday after the Feast of Pentecost inclusively: Solemn Tone, p. 78; Simple Tone, p. 78

ANTIPHON

Queen of heaven, rejoice, alleluia;
For He whom thou didst merit to bear, alleluia,
Has risen as He said, alleluia:
Pray for us to God, alleluia.

℣. Rejoice and be glad, O Virgin Mary, alleluia!
℟. Because the Lord is truly risen, alleluia!

Regína cæli, lætáre, allelúia;
Quia quem meruísti portáre, allelúia,
Resurréxit, sicut dixit, allelúia:
Ora pro nobis Deum, allelúia.

℣. Gaude et lætáre, Virgo María, allelúia.
℟. Quia surréxit Dóminus vere, allelúia.

Collect

Let us pray. O God, who by the Resurrection of Thy Son, our Lord Jesus Christ, didst vouchsafe to make glad the whole world; grant, we beseech Thee, that through the intercession of the Virgin Mary, His Mother, we may lay hold on the joys of eternal life. Through the same Christ our Lord. ℟. Amen.

Orémus. Deus, qui per resurrectiónem Fílii tui, Dómini nostri Jesu Christi, mundum lætificáre dignátus es: præsta, quaésumus; ut per ejus Genetrícem Vírginem Maríam, perpétuæ capiámus gáudia vitæ. Per eúndem Christum Dóminum nostrum.

℟. Amen.

IV

From First Vespers of the Feast of the Blessed Trinity to None on Saturday before the First Sunday of Advent: Solemn Tone, p. 70; Simple Tone, p. 71.

ANTIPHON

HAIL, holy Queen, Mother of mercy, our life, our sweetness, and our hope. To thee do we cry, poor banished children of Eve; to thee do we send up our sighs, mourning and weeping in this valley of tears. Turn, then, most gracious Advocate, thine eyes of mercy towards us; and after this our exile, show unto us the blessed fruit of thy womb, Jesus. O clement, O loving, O sweet Virgin Mary.

℣. Pray for us, O holy Mother of God.
℟. That we may be made worthy of the promises of Christ.

SALVE Regína, Mater misericórdiæ, vita dulcédo, et spes nostra, salve. Ad te clamámus, éxsules fílii Hevæ. Ad te suspirámus, geméntes et flentes in hac lacrimárum valle. Eia ergo, advocáta nostra, illos tuos misericórdes óculos ad nos convérte. Et Jesum, benedíctum fructum ventris tui, nobis post hoc exsílium, osténde. O clemens, O pia, O dulcis Virgo María.

℣. Ora pro nobis, sancta Dei Génitrix.
℟. Ut digni efficiámur promissiónibus Christi.

Collect

Let us pray. O almighty and everlasting God, who, by the co-operation of the Holy Ghost, didst prepare the body and soul of Mary, glorious Virgin and Mother, to become the worthy habitation of Thy Son: grant that we may be delivered from present evils, and from everlasting death, by her gracious intercession, in whose commemoration we rejoice. Through the same Christ our Lord. ℟. Amen.

Orémus. Omnípotens sempitérne Deus, qui gloriósæ Vírginis Matris Maríæ corpus et ánimam, ut dignum Fílii tui habitáculum éffici mererétur, Spíritu Sancto cooperánte, præparásti: da, ut, cuius commemoratióne lætámur, eius pia intercessióne, ab instántibus malis et a morte perpétua liberémur. Per eúndem Christum Dóminum nostrum.

℟. Amen

Then after the final antiphon with its verse and collect, the conclusion is:

℣. May the divine assistance remain always with us.
℟. Amen.

℣. Divínum auxílium máneat semper nobíscum.
℟. Amen.

V

Alternative option for the antiphons outside Eastertide: p. 82.

ANTIPHON

WE fly to thy patronage, O holy Mother of God; despise not our petitions in our necessities, but deliver us always from all dangers, O glorious and blessed Virgin.

SUB tuum præsídium confúgimus, sancta Dei Génitrix : nostras deprecatiónes ne despícias in necessitátibus: sed a perículis cunctis líbera nos semper, Virgo gloriósa et benedícta.

I. Antiphon **Alma Redemptoris Mater**, Solemn Tone

From Vespers of Saturday before the First Sunday of Advent to Second Vespers of the Purification.

Ant. 5.

Alma * Redemptóris Mater, quæ pérvia cæli porta manes, Et stella maris, Succúrre cadénti súrgere qui curat pópulo: Tu quæ genuísti, natúra mirán-te, tuum sanctum Genitórem: Virgo prius ac postérius, Gabriélis ab ore sumens illud Ave, * peccatórum miserére.

Antiphons of the Blessed Virgin

I. Antiphon **Alma Redemptoris Mater**, Simple Tone

From Vespers of Saturday before the First Sunday of Advent to Second Vespers of the Purification.

Ant. 5.

A L- ma * Redemptó-ris Ma-ter, quæ pérvi- a cæ-li porta manes, Et stella ma-ris, succúrre cadénti súrge-re qui cu-rat pópu-lo : Tu quæ genu- í- sti, na-tú-ra mi-ránte, tu- um sanctum Geni-tórem : Virgo pri- us ac posté-ri- us, Gabri- é- lis ab o-re sumens illud Ave, pecca-tórum mi-se-ré- re.

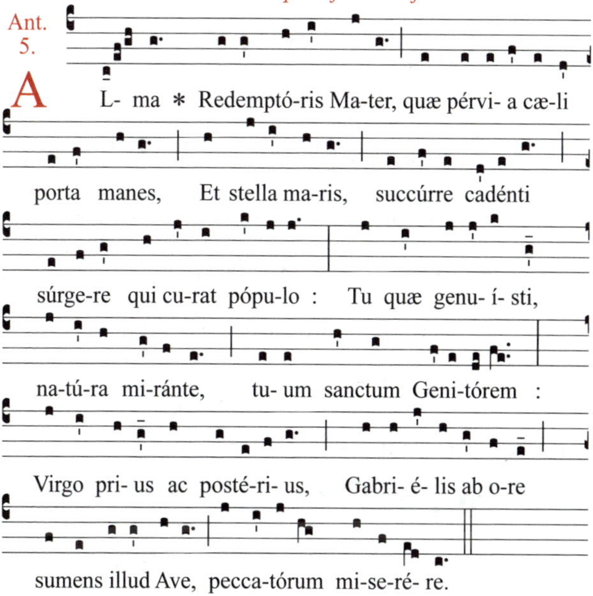

During Advent:
℣. Angelus Dómini nuntiávit Maríæ.
℟. Et concépit de Spíritu Sancto.
Orémus. p. 69.

From 1st Vespers of Christmas to 2nd Vespers of the Purification:
℣. Post partum Virgo invioláta permansísti.
℟. Dei Génitrix intercéde pro nobis.

II. Antiphon Ave Regina Cælorum, Solemn Tone

From Compline of February 2 (even if the Feast of the Purification be transferred) until Compline of Wednesday in Holy Week.

Ave * Regína cælórum, Ave Dómina Angelórum : Salve radix, salve porta, Ex qua mundo lux est orta : Gaude Virgo gloriósa, Super omnes speciósa : Vale, o valde decóra, Et pro nobis Christum * exóra.

II. Antiphon Ave Regina Cælorum, Simple Tone

From Compline of February 2 (even if the Feast of the Purification be transferred) until Compline of Wednesday in Holy Week.

Ant. 6.

A-ve Regína cæ-lórum, * Ave Dómina Ange-lórum : Salve ra-dix, sal-ve porta, Ex qua mundo lux est orta : Gau-de Vírgo glo-ri- ó-sa, Su- per omnes spe-ci- ó-sa : Va-le, o valde de-có- ra, Et pro no- bis Christum exó- ra.

℣. Dignáre me laudáre te Virgo sacráta.
℟. Da mihi virtútem contra hostes tuos.
Orémus. p. 71.

III. Antiphon **Regina Cæli**, Solemn Tone

*From Compline of Easter Sunday to Compline of
Friday after the Feast of Pentecost inclusively.*

Ant. 6.

R̲egína cæli * lætáre, allelúia : Quia quem meruísti portáre, allelúia : Resurréxit, sicut dixit, allelúia : Ora pro nobis Deum, alle- * ** lúia.

III. Antiphon **Regina Cæli**, Simple Tone

*From Compline of Easter Sunday to Compline of
Friday after the Feast of Pentecost inclusively.*

Ant. 6.

R̲egína cæli * lætáre, allelúia : Quia quem merui-ísti portáre, allelúia : Resurréxit, sicut dixit,

alle - lú-ia : Ora pro no-bis De-um, alle- lú - ia.

℣. Gáude et lætáre Vírgo María, allelúia.
℟. Quia surréxit Dóminus vere, allelúia.
Orémus. p. 72.

IV. Antiphon Salve Regina, Solemn Tone

From First Vespers of the Feast of the Blessed Trinity to None on Saturday before the First Sunday of Advent.

Ant. 6.

S Al- ve, *Re-gí- na, ma-ter mi- se-ri-córdi- æ:

Vi- ta, dulcé- do, et spes nostra, sal- ve. Ad te

clamá-mus, éxsu-les, fí-li- i He-væ Ad te suspirámus,

geméntes et flen- tes in hac lacrimá-rum valle.

E- ia ergo, Advocá- ta nostra, illos tu- os

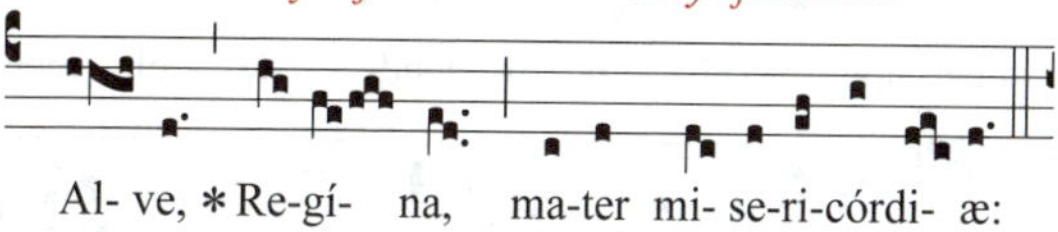

misericórdes óculos ad nos convérte. Et Jesum, benedíctum fructum ventris tui, nobis post hoc exsílium osténde. O clemens : O pia : O dulcis ∗ Virgo María.

IV. Antiphon Salve Regina, Simple Tone

From First Vespers of the Feast of the Blessed Trinity to None on Saturday before the First Sunday of Advent.

Ant. 5.

Salve, Regína, ∗ mater misericórdiæ : Vita, dulcédo, et spes nostra, salve. Ad te clamámus, éxsules, fílii Hevæ Ad te

Antiphons of the Blessed Virgin

suspi-rámus, gemén-tes et flentes in hac lacrimá-rum valle. E-ia ergo, Advocá-ta nostra, il-los tu- os mi-se-ri-córdes ócu-los ad nos convér- te. Et Je-sum, bene-díctum fructum ventris tu- i, nobis post hoc exsí- li- um osténde. O clemens : O pi- a : O dulcis * Virgo Ma-rí- a.

℣. Ora pro nobis, sancta Dei Génitrix.
℞. Ut digni efficiámur promissiónibus Christi.
Orémus. p. 73.

V. Antiphon Sub Tuum Præsidium

Alternative option for the antiphons outside of Eastertide.

Ant. 7.

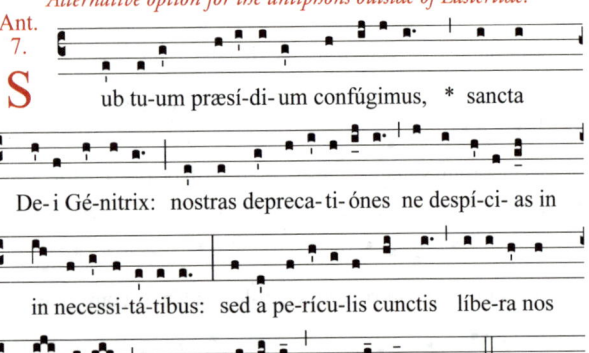

Sub tuum præsídium confúgimus, * sancta Dei Génitrix: nostras deprecatiónes ne despícias in in necessitátibus: sed a perículis cunctis líbera nos semper, Virgo gloriósa et benedícta.

Tu es gaudium et laetitia. Tu es iustitia et temperantia.
Thou art joy and gladness. Thou art justice and temperance.

St. Francis Receiving the Stigmata

Philadelphia, Free Library of Philadelphia, Lewis E 113, fol. 59v.

St. Francis's Little Office of the Passion

Ordinary

For all of the hours, the office opens and proceeds as follows, beginning with either a simple Pater Noster or the following expanded version of Francis's own composition:

OUR **Father**, most holy, our Creator, Redeemer, Savior, and Comforter.

Who art in Heaven, in the angels and in the saints illuminating them unto knowledge, for Thou, O Lord, art light; inflaming them into love, for Thou, O Lord, art Love; dwelling in them and filling them with blessedness, for Thou, O Lord, art the highest Good, the eternal Good from whom is all good and without whom is no good.

Hallowed be Thy Name: may Thy knowledge shine in us that we may know the breadth of Thy benefits, the length of Thy promises, the height of Thy

SANCTÍSSIME *Pater Noster*, Creátor, Redémptor, Salvátor et Consolátor noster.

Qui es in cælis, in ángelis et in sanctis, illúminans eos ad cognitiónem, quia tu, Dómine, lux es; inflámmans ad amórem, quia tu, Dómine, amor es; inhábitans et implens eos ad beatitúdinem, quia tu, Dómine, summum bonum es, ætérnum bonum, a quo omne bonum sine quo nullum bonum.

Sanctificétur nomen tuum: clarificétur in nobis notítia tua, ut cognoscámus, quæ sit latitúdo beneficiórum tuórum, longitúdo promissórum tuórum,

majesty, and the depth of Thy judgments.

Thy Kingdom come, that Thou may reign in us by grace and make us come to Thy Kingdom, where there is the clear vision of Thee, the perfect love of Thee, the blessed company of Thee, the eternal enjoyment of Thee.

Thy will be done on earth as it is in heaven, that we may love Thee with the whole heart by always thinking of Thee; with the whole soul by always desiring Thee; with the whole mind by directing all our intentions to Thee and seeking Thy honor in all things and with all our strength, by spending all the powers and senses of the body and soul in the service of Thy love and not in anything else; and that we may love our neighbors even as ourselves, drawing to the best of our power all to Thy love; rejoicing in the good of others as in our own and suffering with them in misfortunes and giving offense to no one.

Our daily bread, Thy beloved Son, our Lord Jesus Christ, ***give us this day,*** through memory and understanding and reverence for the love which He had for us and for those things

sublímitas maiestátis et profúnditas iudiciórum.

Advéniat regnum tuum, ut tu regnes in nobis per grátiam et fácias nos veníre ad regnum tuum, ubi est tui vísio manifésta, tui diléctio perfécta, tui socíetas beáta, tui fruítio sempitérna.

Fiat volúntas tua sicut in cælo et in terra, ut amémus te ex toto corde te semper cogitándo, ex toto ánima te semper desiderándo, ex tota mente omnes intentiónes nostras ad te dirigéndo et honórem tuum in ómnibus quæréndo, et ex ómnibus víribus nostris omnes vires et sensus ánimæ et córporis in obséquium tui amóris et non in álio expendéndo; et próximos nostros amémus sicut et nosmetípsos, omnes ad amórem tuum pro víribus trahéndo, de bonis aliórum sicut de nostris gaudéndo et in malis compatiéndo et némini ullam offensiónem dando.

Panem nostrum quotidiánum, diléctum Fílium tuum, Dóminum nostrum Iesum Christum, ***da nobis hódie***, in memóriam et intelligéntiam et reveréntiam amóris, quem ad

which He said, and did, and suffered, for us.

And forgive us our trespasses, by Thy ineffable mercy in virtue of the Passion of Thy Beloved Son, our Lord Jesus Christ, and through the merits and intercession of the most Blessed Virgin Mary and all of Thy elect.

As we forgive them that trespass against us, and what we do not fully forgive, do Thou, O Lord, make us fully forgive, that for Thy sake we may truly love our enemies and devoutly intercede for them with Thee; that we may render no evil for evil, but in Thee may strive to do good to all.

And lead us not into temptation, hidden or manifest, sudden or persistent.

But deliver us from evil, past, present, and to come. Amen.

Glory be to the Father, and to the Son, and to the Holy Ghost; as it was in the beginning, is now, and will be forever. Amen.

nos hábuit, et eórum quæ pro nobis dixit, fecit, et sústulit.

Et dimítte nobis débita nostra, per tuam misericórdiam ineffábilem, per passiónis dilécti Fílii tui Dómini nostri Iesu Christi virtútem et per beatíssimæ Maríæ Vírginis et ómnium electórum tuórum mérita et intercessiónem.

Sicut et nos dimíttimus debitóribus nostris, et quod non plene dimíttimus, tu, Dómine, fac nos plene dimíttere, ut inimícos propter te veráciter diligámus et pro eis apud te devóte intercedámus, nulli malum pro malo reddámus et ómnibus in te prodésse studeámus.

Et ne nos indúcas in tentatiónem, occúltam vel maniféstam, súbitam vel importúnam.

Sed líbera nos a malo, prætérito, præsénti, et futúram. Amen.

Glória Patri, et Fílio, et Spirítui Sancto. Sicut erat in princípio, et nunc, et semper, et in sǽcula sæculórum. Amen.

PRAISES TO BE SAID AT ALL HOURS

HOLY, Holy, Holy, Lord God Almighty, who is and who was and who is to come:

Let us praise and exalt Him above all forever.

Worthy art Thou, O Lord, our God, to receive praise and glory and honor and benediction:

Let us praise and exalt Him above all forever.

The Lamb that was slain is worthy to receive power and divinity and wisdom and strength and honor and benediction:

Let us praise and exalt Him above all forever.

Let us bless the Father and the Son with the Holy Ghost:

Let us praise and exalt Him above all forever.

All you works of the Lord, bless the Lord:

Let us praise and exalt Him above all forever.

Give praise to God all you His servants and you that fear Him, little and great:

Let us praise and exalt Him above all forever.

Let the heavens and earth praise Him, the Glorious: and every creature which is in heaven and on earth and under the

SANCTUS, sanctus sanctus, Dóminus Deus omnípotens, qui est qui erat et qui ventúrus est:

Laudémus et superexaltémus eum in sǽcula.

Dignus es, Dómine Deus noster, accípere laudem, glóriam et honórem et benedictiónem:

Laudémus et superexaltémus eum in sǽcula.

Dignus est agnus, qui occísus est, accípere virtútem et divinitátem et sapiéntiam et fortitúdinem et honórem et glóriam et benedictiónem:

Laudémus et superexaltémus eum in sǽcula.

Benedicámus Patrem et Fílium cum Sancto Spíritu:

Laudémus et superexaltémus eum in sǽcula.

Benedícite ómnia ópera Dómini Dómino:

Laudémus et superexaltémus eum in sǽcula.

Laudem dícite Deo nostro omnes servi eius et qui timétis Deum, pusílli et magni:

Laudémus et superexaltémus eum in sǽcula.

Laudent eum gloriósum cæli et terra: et omnis creatúra, quæ in cælo est et super terram et quæ subtus terram, mare et quæ

earth, in the seas and all that are in them:

Let us praise and exalt Him above all forever.

Glory be to the Father, and to the Son, and to the Holy Ghost:

Let us praise and exalt Him above all forever.

As it was in the beginning, is now, and ever shall be, world without end. Amen.

Let us praise and exalt Him above all forever.

in eo sunt:

Laudémus et superexaltémus eum in sǽcula.

Glória Patri et Fílio et Spirítui Sancto:

Laudémus et superexaltémus eum in sǽcula.

Sicut erat in princípio, et nunc, et semper, et in sǽcula sæculórum. Amen.

Laudémus et superexaltémus eum in sǽcula.

Oratio

Almighty, most holy, most high, and supreme God, highest good, all good, wholly good, who alone art good. To Thee we render all praise, all glory, all thanks, all honor, all blessing, and we shall always refer all good to Thee. Amen.

Omnípotens, sanctíssime, altíssime et summe Deus, summum bonum, omne bonum, totum bonum, qui solus es bonus, tibi reddámus omnem laudem, omnem glóriam, omnem grátiam, omnem honórem, omnem benedictiónem et ómnia bona tibi referámus semper. Amen.

Ant. Holy Virgin Mary, there is none like unto thee born in the world among women, daughter and handmaid of the most high King, the heavenly Father, Mother of our most holy Lord Jesus Christ, Spouse of the Holy Ghost; pray for us, with St. Michael the Archangel, and all the powers of heaven, and all the saints, before thy most

Ant. Sancta María virgo, non est tibi símilis nata in mundo in muliéribus, fília et ancílla altíssimi Regis Patris cæléstis, mater sanctíssimi Dómini nostri Iesu Christi, sponsa Spíritus Sancti; ora pro nobis cum Sancto Michaéle archángelo et ómnibus virtútibus cælórum et ómnibus sanctis apud tuum sanctíssimum diléctum Fílium, Dóminum no-

holy, beloved Son, our Lord and Teacher. *Glory be,* etc.

strum et Magístrum. *Glória Patri,* etc.

Then is said one of the psalms of Saint Francis, according to the season and hour, followed by the Glória Patri:

see PROPERS, *p. 92.*

The office then continues and concludes:

Ant. Holy Virgin Mary, there is none like unto thee born in the world among women, daughter and handmaid of the most high King, the heavenly Father, Mother of our most holy Lord Jesus Christ, Spouse of the Holy Ghost; pray for us, with St. Michael the Archangel, and all the powers of heaven, and all the saints, before thy most holy, beloved Son, our Lord and Teacher. *Glory be,* etc.

Ant. Sancta María virgo, non est tibi símilis nata in mundo in muliéribus, fília et ancílla altíssimi Regis Patris cæléstis, mater sanctíssimi Dómini nostri Iesu Christi, sponsa Spíritus Sancti; ora pro nobis cum Sancto Michaéle archángelo et ómnibus virtútibus cælórum et ómnibus sanctis apud tuum sanctíssimum diléctum Fílium, Dóminum nostrum et Magístrum. *Glória Patri,* etc.

Blessing

Let us bless the Lord God living and true; let us refer praise, glory, honor, blessing and all good to Him always. Amen. Amen. Fiat. Fiat.

Benedicámus Dómino Deo vivo et vero: laudem, glóriam, honórem, benedictiónem et ómnia bona referámus ei semper. Amen. Amen. Fiat. Fiat.

Following the hour of compline, one may say Francis's Salutation to the Blessed Virgin, below, as the Marian antiphon.

SALUTATION TO THE BLESSED VIRGIN

HAIL, Lady, Holy Queen, Mary mother of God, you who are the virgin made Church, chosen by the most Holy Father in heaven, whom he

AVE Dómina, sancta Regína, sancta, Dei génetrix María, quæ es virgo Ecclésia facta, et elécta a sanctíssimo Patre de cælo, quam consecrávit cum

consecrated with His most holy beloved Son, and with the Holy Spirit the Paraclete, in whom there was and is all fullness of grace and every good. Hail His palace; hail His tabernacle; hail His dwelling. Hail His robe; hail His handmaid; hail His mother. Hail all you holy virtues, which are poured into the hearts of the faithful through the grace and illumination of the Holy Spirit, that from being unfaithful, you make them faithful to God.

sanctíssimo dilécto Fílio suo et Spíritu Sancto Paráclito, in qua fuit et est omnis plenitúdo grátiæ et omne bonum. Ave palátium eius; ave tabernáculum eius; ave domus eius. Ave vestiméntum eius; ave ancílla eius; ave mater eius. Ave sanctæ virtútes, quæ per grátiam et illuminatiónem Spíritus Sancti infundímini in corda fidélium, ut de infidélibus fidéles Deo faciátis.

Propers

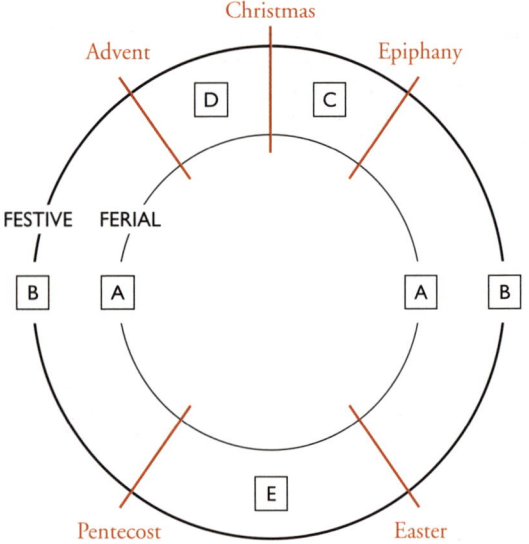

Propers

	Com-pline	Lauds	Prime	Terce	Sext	None	Vespers
Cycle A	I	II	III	IV	V	VI	VII
Cycle B	VIII	IX	III	X	XI	XII	VII
Cycle D	XIII	XIV	III	X	XI	XII	VII
Cycle C	VIII	XV	III	XV	XV	XV	XV
Cycle E	VIII	IX	III	IX	IX	IX	VII

These fifteen psalms are all Scriptural arrangements of St. Francis's own composition; they are designated here by Roman numerals to distinguish them from the numbering of the Psalter. St. Francis's slight deviations from or additions to the Vulgate are marked by italics. Whereas St. Bonaventure's Office of the Passion ended at Compline with Christ's entombment, St. Francis's Passion narrative begins at Compline with the Agony in the Garden, hence the designation of Psalm I. Cycles A and B are said from Epiphany to Easter, including during Lent, and from after Pentecost to the start of Advent. Cycle A is reserved for weekdays, while Cycle B is said on Sundays and feast days. Cycle D is said during Advent; Cycle C, during the Christmas season; and Cycle E, during Paschal time.

PSALM I

Compline, Cycle A

Ps. 55:9	O GOD, I have declared to Thee my life; Thou hast set my tears in Thy sight.
Ps. 40:8, Ps. 70:10	All my enemies devised evils against me: they have consulted together.
Ps. 108:5	And they have repaid me evil for good: and hatred for my love.
Ps. 108:4	Instead of making me a return of love they detracted me: but I gave myself to prayer.
Jn. 17:11, Mt. 11:25, Ps. 21:12	*My* holy Father, *King* of heaven and earth, depart not from me: for tribulation is near and there is none to help.
Ps. 55:10	My enemies shall be turned back: in whatsoever day I shall call upon Thee, behold I know that Thou art my God.
Ps. 37:12	My friends and my neighbors have drawn near and stood against me: and they that were near me stood far off.
Ps. 87:9	Thou hast put away my acquaintance far from me, they have set me an abomination to them: I was delivered up and came not forth.
Jn. 17:11, Ps. 21:20	Holy Father, remove not Thy help from me: my God, look toward my help.
Ps. 37:23	Attend unto my help, O Lord, the God of my salvation.

Glory be to the Father and to the Son and to the Holy Ghost.

As it was in the beginning, is now, and ever shall be, world without end. Amen.

PSALM I
Compline, Cycle A

DEUS vitam meam annuntiávi tibi: posuísti lácrymas meas in conspéctu tuo. *Ps. 55:9*

Omnes inimíci mei advérsum me cogitábant mala mihi: consílium fecérunt in unum. *Ps. 40:8, Ps. 70:10*

Et posuérunt advérsum me mala pro bonis: et ódium pro dilectióne mea. *Ps. 108:5*

Pro eo, ut me dilígerent, detrahébant mihi: ego autem orábam. *Ps. 108:4*

Mi Pater sancte, *Rex* cæli et terræ, ne discésseris a me: quóniam tribulátio próxima est, et non est qui ádiuvet. *Jn. 17:11, Mt. 11:25, Ps. 21:12*

Converténtur inimíci mei retrórsum: in quacúmque die invocávero te, ecce cognóvi, quóniam Deus meus es. *Ps. 55:10*

Amíci mei et próximi mei advérsum me appropinquavérunt et stetérunt: et próximi mei de longe stetérunt. *Ps. 37:12*

Longe fecísti notos a me, posuérunt me abominatiónem sibi: tráditus sum et non egrediébar. *Ps. 87:9*

Pater sancte, ne elongáveris auxílium tuum a me: Deus meus, ad auxílium meum réspice. *Jn. 17:11, Ps. 21:20*

Inténde in adiutórium meum: Dómine Deus salútis meæ. *Ps. 37:23*

Glória Patri, et Fílio, et Spirítui Sancto.

Sicut erat in princípio, et nunc, et semper, et in sǽcula sæculórum. Amen.

PSALM II

Lauds, Cycle A

Ps. 87:2   O LORD, the God of my salvation: I have cried in the day and night before Thee.

Ps. 87:3   Let my prayer come in before Thee: incline Thy ear to my petition.

Ps. 68:19   Attend to my soul and deliver it: save me because of my enemies.

Ps. 21:20   For Thou art He that hast drawn me out of the womb, my hope from the breasts of my mother: I was cast upon Thee from the womb.

Ps. 21:11-12   From my mother's womb Thou art my God: depart not from me.

Ps. 68:20   Thou knowest my reproach and my confusion: and my shame.

Ps. 68:21   In Thy sight are all they that afflict me: my heart hath expected reproach and misery.

Ps. 85:14   And I looked for one that would grieve together with me, but there was none: and for one that would comfort me and I found none.

Ps. 87:5-6   O God, the wicked are risen up against me: and the assembly of the mighty have sought my soul; and they have not set Thee before their eyes.

Ps. 43:5   I am counted among them that go down to the pit: I am become as a man without help, free among the dead.

Ps. 37:23   *Thou art my most holy Father,* my king and my God. Attend unto my help, O Lord God of my salvation.

PSALM II
Lauds, Cycle A

DÓMINE Deus salútis meæ: in die clamávi et nocte coram te. *Ps. 87:2*

Intret in conspéctu tuo orátio mea: inclína aurem tuam ad precem meam. *Ps. 87:3*

Inténde ánimæ meæ et líbera eam: propter inimícos meos éripe me. *Ps. 68:19*

Quóniam tu es, qui abstraxísti me de ventre, spes mea ab ubéribus matris meæ: in te proiéctus sum ex útero. *Ps. 21:20*

De ventre matris meæ Deus meus es tu: ne discésseris a me. *Ps. 21:11-12*

Tu scis impropérium meum et confusiónem meam: et reveréntiam meam. *Ps. 68:20*

In conspéctu tuo sunt omnes, qui tríbulant me: impropérium exspectávit cor meum et misériam. *Ps. 68:21*

Et sustínui, qui simul contristarétur, et non fuit: et qui consolarétur, et non invéni. *Ps. 85:14*

Deus, iníqui insurrexérunt super me: et synagóga poténtium quæsiérunt ánimam meam: et non proposuérunt te in conspéctu suo. *Ps. 87:5-6*

Æstimátus sum cum descendéntibus in lacum: factus sum sicut homo sine adiutório, inter mórtuos liber. *Ps. 43:5*

Tu es sanctíssimus Pater meus: Rex meus et Deus meus. *Ps. 37:23*
Inténde in adiutórium meum: Dómine Deus salútis meæ.

PSALM III

Prime, all cycles

Ps. 56:1   HAVE mercy on me, O God, have mercy on me: for my soul trusteth in Thee.

Ps. 56:2   And in the shadow of Thy wings will I hope: until iniquity pass away.

Ps. 56:3   I will cry to *my most holy Father,* the Most High: to God, who hath done good to me.

Ps. 56:4   He hath sent from heaven and delivered me; He hath made them a reproach that trod upon me.

Ps. 56:4, Ps. 17:18   God hath sent His power and His truth: He delivered me from my strongest enemies and from them that hated me, for they were too strong for me.

Ps. 56:7   They prepared a snare for my feet; and they bowed down before my soul.

Ps. 56:7   They dug a pit before my face: and they are fallen into it.

Ps. 56:8   My heart is ready, O God, my heart is ready; I will sing, and rehearse a psalm.

Ps. 56:9   Arise, O my glory, arise psaltery and harp: I will arise early.

Ps. 56:10   I will give praise to Thee, O Lord, among the people: I will sing a psalm to Thee among the nations;

Ps. 56:11   For Thy mercy is magnified even to the heavens; and Thy truth unto the clouds.

Ps. 56:12   Be Thou exalted, O God, above all the heavens; and Thy glory above all the earth.

PSALM III

Prime, all cycles

MISERÉRE mei, Deus, miserére mei: quóniam in te confídit ánima mea. — *Ps. 56:1*

Et in umbra alárum tuárum sperábo: donec tránseat iníquitas. — *Ps. 56:2*

Clamábo ad *sanctíssimum Patrem meum* altíssimum: Deum, qui benefécit mihi. — *Ps. 56:3*

Misit de cælo et liberávit me: dedit in oppróbrium conculcántes me. — *Ps. 56:4*

Misit Deus manum suam et veritátem suam: ánimam meam erípuit de inimícis meis fortíssimis et ab his qui odérunt me, quóniam confortáti sunt super me. — *Ps. 56:4, Ps. 17:18*

Láqueum paravérunt pédibus meis: et incurvavérunt ánimam meam. — *Ps. 56:7*

Fodérunt ante fáciem meam fóveam: et incidérunt in eam. — *Ps. 56:7*

Parátum cor meum, Deus, parátum cor meum: cantábo et psalmum dicam. — *Ps. 56:8*

Exsúrge, glória mea, exsúrge, psaltérium et cíthara: exsúrgam dilúculo. — *Ps. 56:9*

Confitébor tibi in pópulis, Dómine: et psalmum dicam tibi in géntibus. — *Ps. 56:10*

Quóniam magnificáta est usque ad cælos misericórdia tua: et usque ad nubes véritas tua. — *Ps. 56:11*

Exaltáre super cælos, Deus: et super omnem terram glória tua. — *Ps. 56:12*

PSALM IV

Terce, Cycle A

Ps. 55:2   HAVE mercy on me, O God, for man hath trodden me underfoot: all the day long he hath afflicted me, fighting against me.

Ps. 55:3   My enemies have trodden on me all the day long: for they are many that make war against me.

Ps. 40:8-9   All my enemies devised evils against me: they determined against me an unjust word.

Ps. 70:10   They that watched my soul: have consulted together.

Ps. 40:7   They went out: and spoke to the same purpose.

Ps. 21:8   All they that saw me have laughed me to scorn: they have spoken with the lips and wagged the head.

Ps. 21:7   But I am a worm and no man, a reproach of men and outcast of the people.

Ps. 30:12   I am become a reproach among all my enemies and very much to my neighbors; and a fear to my acquaintance.

Jn. 17:11, Ps. 21:20   Holy Father, remove not Thy help far from me; my God, look toward my defense.

Ps. 37:23   Attend unto my help, O Lord God of my salvation.

PSALM IV
Terce, Cycle A

MISERÉRE mei, Deus, quóniam conculcávit me homo: tota die impúgnans tribulávit me. *Ps. 55:2*

Conculcavérunt me inimíci mei tota die: quóniam multi bellántes advérsum me. *Ps. 55:3*

Omnes inimíci mei advérsum me cogitábant mala mihi: verbum iníquum constituérunt advérsum me. *Ps. 40:8-9*

Qui custodiébant ánimam meam: consílium fecérunt in unum. *Ps. 70:10*

Egrediebátur foras: et loquebántur in idípsum. *Ps. 40:7*

Omnes vidéntes me derisérunt me: locúti sunt lábiis et movérunt caput. *Ps. 21:8*

Ego autem sum vermis et non homo: oppróbrium hóminum et abiéctio plebis. *Ps. 21:7*

Super omnes inimícos meos factus sum oppróbrium vicínis meis valde: et timor notis meis. *Ps. 30:12*

Pater sancte, ne elongáveris auxílium tuum a me: ad defensiónem meam cónspice. *Jn. 17:11, Ps. 21:20*

Inténde in adiutórium meum: Dómine Deus salútis meæ. *Ps. 37:23*

PSALM V

Sext, Cycle A

Ps. 141:2	I CRIED to the Lord with my voice: with my voice I made my supplication to the Lord.
Ps. 141:3	I pour out my prayer in His sight: and before Him I declare my trouble.
Ps. 141:4	When my spirit failed me: then Thou knewest my paths.
Ps. 141:4	In this way wherein I walked: they have hidden a snare for me.
Ps. 141:5	I looked on my right hand, and beheld: and there was no one that would know me.
Ps. 141:5	Flight hath failed me: and there is no one that hath regard to my soul.
Ps. 68:8	Because for Thy sake I have borne reproach: shame hath covered my face.
Ps. 68:9	I am become a stranger to my brethren: and an alien to the sons of my mother.
Jn. 17:11, Ps. 68:10	Holy Father, the zeal of Thy house hath consumed me: and the reproaches of them that reproached me are fallen upon me.
Ps. 34:15	And they rejoiced against me and gathered together: scourges were gathered together against me, and I knew not.
Ps. 68:5	They are multiplied above the hairs of my head: who hate me without cause.
Ps. 68:5	My enemies are grown strong who have wrongfully persecuted me: then did I pay that which I took not away.
Ps. 34:11	Unjust witnesses rising up: have asked me things I knew not.
Ps. 34:12, Ps. 37:21	They repaid me evil for good and detracted me: because I followed goodness.
Ps. 43:5	Thou art *my Father most holy*: my King and my God.
Ps. 37:23	Attend unto my help: O Lord God of my salvation.

PSALM V
Sext, Cycle A

VOCE mea ad Dóminum clamávi: voce mea ad Dóminum deprecátus sum. — *Ps. 141:2*

Effúndo in conspéctu eius oratiónem meam: et tribulatiónem meam ante ipsum pronúntio. — *Ps. 141:3*

In deficiéndo ex me spíritum meum: et tu cognovísti sémitas meas. — *Ps. 141:4*

In via hac, qua ambulábam: abscondérunt láqueum mihi. — *Ps. 141:4*

Considerábam ad déxteram et vidébam: et non erat qui cognósceret me. — *Ps. 141:5*

Périit fuga a me: et non est qui requírat ánimam meam. — *Ps. 141:5*

Quóniam propter te sustínui oppróbrium: opéruit confúsio fáciem meam. — *Ps. 68:8*

Extráneus factus sum frátribus meis: et peregrínus fíliis matris meæ. — *Ps. 68:9*

Pater sancte, zelus domus tuæ comédit me: et oppróbria exprobrántium tibi cecidérunt super me. — *Jn. 17:11, Ps. 68:10*

Et advérsum me lætáti sunt et convenérunt: congregáta sunt super me flagélla, et ignorávi. — *Ps. 34:15*

Multiplicáti sunt super capíllos cápitis mei: qui odérunt me gratis. — *Ps. 68:5*

Confortáti sunt qui persecúti sunt me inimíci mei iniúste: quæ non rápui tunc exsolvébam. — *Ps. 68:5*

Surgéntes testes iníqui: quæ ignorábam, interrogábant me. — *Ps. 34:11*

Retribuébant mihi mala pro nobis et detrahébant mihi: quóniam sequébar bonitátem. — *Ps. 34:12, Ps. 37:21*

Tu es *sanctíssimus Pater meus*: Rex meus et Deus meus. — *Ps. 43:5*

Inténde in adiutórium meum: Dómine, Deus salútis meæ. — *Ps. 37:23*

PSALM VI

None, Cycle A

Lam. 1:12	O ALL you that pass by: attend and see if there be any sorrow like to my sorrow.
Ps. 21:17	For many dogs have encompassed me: the council of the malignant hath besieged me.
Ps. 21:18-19	They looked and stared upon me: they parted my garments among them and upon my vesture cast lots.
Ps. 21:17-18	They have pierced my hands and my feet: they numbered all my bones.
Ps. 21:14	They have opened their mouths against me: as a lion ravening and roaring.
Ps. 21:15	I am poured out like water and all my bones are scattered.
Ps. 21:15	My heart is become like melting-wax: in the midst of my bowels.
Ps. 21:16	My strength is dried up like a potsherd: and my tongue hath cleaved to my jaws.
Ps. 68:22	And they gave me gall for my food: and in my thirst they gave me vinegar to drink.
Ps. 21:16, Ps. 68:27	And Thou hast brought me into the dust of death: and they have added to the grief of my wounds.
Ps. 3:6, Ps. 72:24	I slept and rose again; and my *most holy Father* received me with glory.
Jn. 17:11, Ps. 72:24	Holy Father, Thou hast held my right hand; and by Thy will Thou hast conducted me and hast received me with glory.
Ps. 72:25	For what am I in heaven: and besides Thee what do I desire on earth?
Ps. 45:11	Be still and see that I am God, saith the Lord: I will be exalted among the nations and I will be exalted in the earth.
Lk. 1:68, Ps. 33:23	Blessed be the God of Israel, who has redeemed the souls of His servants with His own most holy Blood: and none of them that trust in Him shall offend.
Ps. 95:13	And we know that He cometh: for *He will come again to judge justice.*

PSALM VI
None, Cycle A

O VOS omnes, qui transítis per viam: atténdite et vidéte, si est dolor sicut dolor meus. *Lam. 1:12*

Quóniam circumdedérunt me canes multi: consílium malignántium obsédit me. *Ps. 21:17*

Ipsi vero consideravérunt et inspexérunt me: divisérunt sibi vestiménta mea et super vestem meam misérunt sortem. *Ps. 21:18-19*

Fodérunt manus meas et pedes meos: et dinumeravérunt ómnia ossa mea. *Ps. 21:17-18*

Aperuérunt super me os suum: sicut leo rápiens et rúgiens. *Ps. 21:14*

Sicut aqua effúsus sum: et dispérsa sunt ómnia ossa mea. *Ps. 21:15*

Et factum est cor meum tanquam cera liquéscens: in médio ventris mei. *Ps. 21:15*

Áruit tanquam testa virtus mea: et lingua mea adhǽsit fáucibus meis. *Ps. 21:16*

Et dedérunt in escam meam fel: et in siti mea potavérunt me acéto. *Ps. 68:22*

Et in púlverem mortis deduxérunt me: et super dolórem vúlnerum meórum addidérunt. *Ps. 21:16, Ps. 68:27*

Ego dormívi et resurréxi: et *Pater meus sanctíssimus* cum glória suscépit me. *Ps. 3:6, Ps. 72:24*

Pater sancte, tenuísti manum déxteram meam: et in voluntáte tua deduxísti me et cum glória assumpsísti me. *Jn. 17:11, Ps. 72:24*

Quid enim mihi est in cælo: et a te quid vólui super terram? *Ps. 72:25*

Vidéte, vidéte, quóniam ego sum Deus, dicit Dóminus: exaltábor in géntibus et exaltábor in terra. *Ps. 45:11*

Benedíctus Dóminus Deus Israël, qui redémit ánimas servórum suórum de próprio sanctíssimo sánguine suo: et non delínquent omnes, qui sperant in eo. *Lk. 1:68, Ps. 33:23*

Et scimus, quóniam venit: quóniam *véniet iustítiam iudicáre*. *Ps. 95:13*

PSALM VII

Vespers, Cycles A, B, D, and E

Ps. 46:2	O CLAP your hands, all you nations: shout unto God with the voice of joy.
Ps. 46:3	For the Lord is high, terrible: He is a great king over all the earth.
Ps. 73:12	*For the most holy Father of heaven,* our King, before ages: sent His *beloved* Son from on high: and hath wrought salvation in the midst of the earth.
Ps. 95:11-12	Let the heavens rejoice and let the earth be glad, let the sea be moved and the fulness thereof: the fields and all that are in them shall be joyful.
Ps. 95:1	Sing unto *Him* a new canticle: sing unto the Lord, all the earth.
Ps. 95:4	For the Lord is great and exceedingly to be praised: He is to be feared above all gods.
Ps. 95:7-8	Bring to the Lord, O you kindreds of the gentiles, bring to the Lord glory and honor: bring to the Lord glory unto His Name.
Lk. 14:27, Jn. 19:17	*Bring your own bodies* and *bear* His holy *cross*: and follow *His most holy precepts even unto the end.*
Ps. 95:9-10	Let all the earth be moved at His presence: say among the gentiles that the Lord hath reigned.

From the feast of the Ascension until Advent, the following verses are added:

	And He ascended unto heaven; and sitteth at the right hand of the most Holy Father in heaven.
Ps. 56:12	Be Thou exalted, O God, above the heavens; and Thy glory above all the earth.
Ps. 95:13	And we know that He cometh: for He will come to judge *justice*.

PSALM VII

Vespers, Cycles A, B, D, and E

OMNES gentes, pláudite mánibus: iubiláte Deo in voce exsultatiónis. — *Ps. 46:2*

Quóniam Dóminus excélsus, terríbilis: Rex magnus super omnem terram. — *Ps. 46:3*

Quia sanctíssimus Pater de cælo, Rex noster: ante sǽcula misit *diléctum* Fílium suum de alto: et operátus est salútem in médio terræ. — *Ps. 73:12*

Læténtur cæli et exsúltet terra, commoveátur mare et plenitúdo eius: gaudébunt campi et ómnia, quæ in eis sunt. — *Ps. 95:11-12*

Cantáte *ei* cánticum novum: cantáte Dómino omnis terra. — *Ps. 95:1*

Quóniam magnus Dóminus et laudábilis nimis: terríbilis est super omnes deos. — *Ps. 95:4*

Afférte Dómino pátriæ géntium, afférte Dómino glóriam et honórem: afférte Dómino glóriam nómini eius. — *Ps. 95:7-8*

Tóllite córpora vestra et *baiuláte* sanctam crucem eius: et sequímini *usque in finem sanctíssima præcépta eius*. — *Lk. 14:27, Jn. 19:17*

Commoveátur a fácie eius univérsa terra: dícite in géntibus, quia Dóminus regnávit. — *Ps. 95:9-10*

From the feast of the Ascension until Advent, the following verses are added:

Et ascéndit ad cælos et sedet ad déxteram sanctíssimi Patris in cælis.

Exaltáre super cælos Deus: et super omnem terram glória tua. — *Ps. 56:12*

Et scimus quóniam venit: quóniam véniet *iustítiam* iudicáre. — *Ps. 95:13*

PSALM VIII

Compline, Cycles B, C, E

Ps. 69—Deus, in adiutorium

O GOD, come to my assistance: O Lord, make haste to help me.

Let them be confounded and ashamed: that seek my soul,

Let them be turned backward and blush for shame: that desire evils to me,

Let them be presently turned away blushing for shame: that say to me, 'Tis well, 'tis well.

Let all that seek Thee rejoice and be glad in Thee: and let such as love Thy salvation say always, The Lord be magnified.

But I am needy and poor: O God, help me.

Thou art my helper and my deliverer: O Lord, make no delay.

PSALM VIII

Compline, Cycles B, C, E

Ps. 69—Deus, in adiutorium

DEUS, in adiutórium meum inténde: Dómine, ad adiuvándum me festína.

Confundántur, et revereántur: qui quærunt ánimam meam.

Avertántur retrórsum, et erubéscant: qui volunt mihi mala.

Avertántur statim erubescéntes: qui dicunt mihi, Euge, euge.

Exsúltent et læténtur in te omnes qui quærunt te, et dicant semper: Magnificétur Dóminus, qui díligunt salutáre tuum.

Ego vero egénus et pauper sum: Deus, ádiuva me.

Adiútor meus et liberátor meus es tu: Dómine, ne moréris.

PSALM IX

Lauds, Cycles B & E; Terce, Sext, None, Cycle E

Ps. 97:1   SING to the Lord a new canticle: for He hath done wonderful things.

Ps. 97:1   His right hand hath *sacrificed His Son*; and His arm is holy.

Ps. 97:2   The Lord hath made known His salvation: He hath revealed His justice in the sight of the gentiles.

Ps. 41:9   In the daytime the Lord hath commanded His mercy: and a canticle to Him in the night.

Ps. 117:24   This is the day which the Lord hath made: let us rejoice and be glad in it.

Ps. 117:26-27   Blessed be He that cometh in the name of the Lord: the Lord is God and He hath shone upon us.

Ps. 95:11-12   Let the heavens rejoice and let the earth be glad, let the sea be moved and the fulness thereof: the fields shall rejoice and all that are in them.

Ps. 95:7-8   Bring to the Lord, O you kindreds of the gentiles, bring to the Lord glory and honor: bring to the Lord glory unto His Name.

On the feast of the Ascension until Advent, the following verses are added;

Ps. 67:33   Sing to God, you kingdoms of the earth: sing to the Lord:

Ps. 67:34   Sing to God, who mounteth above the heaven of heavens: to the east.

Ps. 67:34-5   Behold He will give to His voice the voice of power, give glory to God for Israel: His magnificence and His power is in the clouds.

Ps. 67:36   God is wonderful in His saints: the God of Israel is He who will give power and strength to His people. Blessed be God.

PSALM IX

Lauds, Cycles B & E; Terce, Sext, None, Cycle E

CANTÁTE Dómino cánticum novum: quia mirabília fecit.	*Ps. 97:1*
Sacrificávit Fílium Suum déxtera eius: et bráchium sanctum eius.	*Ps. 97:1*
Notum fecit Dóminus salutáre suum: in conspéctu géntium revelávit iustítiam suam.	*Ps. 97:2*
In illa die mandávit Dóminus misericórdiam suam: et nocte cánticum eius.	*Ps. 41:9*
Hæc est dies, quam fecit Dóminus: exsultémus et lætémur in ea.	*Ps. 117:24*
Benedíctus qui venit in nómine Dómini: Deus Dóminus, et illúxit nobis.	*Ps. 117:26-27*
Læténtur cæli, et exsúltet terra, commoveátur mare et plenitúdo eius: gaudébunt campi et ómnia, quæ in eis sunt.	*Ps. 95:11-12*
Afférte Dómino pátriæ géntium, afférte Dómino glóriam et honórem: afférte Dómino glóriam nómini eius.	*Ps. 95:7-8*

On the feast of the Ascension until Advent, the following verses are added;

Regna terræ, cantáte Deo: psállite Dómino:	*Ps. 67:33*
Psállite Deo, qui ascéndit super cælum cæli: ad oriéntem.	*Ps. 67:34*
Ecce dabit voci suæ vocem virtútis; date glóriam Deo super Israël: magnificéntia eius et virtus eius in núbibus.	*Ps. 67:34-5*
Mirábilis Deus in sanctis suis: Deus Israël ipse dabit virtútem et fortitúdinem plebi suæ, benedíctus Deus.	*Ps. 67:36*

PSALM X

Terce, Cycles B & D

Ps. 65:1-2   SHOUT with joy to *the Lord*, all the earth, sing a psalm to His name: give glory to His praise.

Ps. 65:3   Say unto God, How terrible are Thy works, O Lord: in the multitude of Thy strength Thy enemies shall lie to thee.

Ps. 65:4   Let all the earth adore Thee and sing to Thee: let it sing a psalm to Thy Name.

Ps. 65:16   Come and hear, all you that fear God: and I will tell you what great things He hath done for my soul.

Ps. 65:17   I cried to him with my mouth: and I extolled him with my tongue.

Ps. 17:7   And He heard my voice from His holy temple: and my cry came before Him.

Ps. 65:8   O bless our God, you gentiles: and make the voice of His praise to be heard.

Ps. 71:17   And in him shall all the tribes of the earth be blessed: all nations shall magnify Him.

Ps. 71:18   Blessed be the Lord God of Israel: who only doth wonderful things.

Ps. 71:19   And blessed be the Name of His majesty forever: and the whole earth shall be filled with his majesty. So be it. So be it.

PSALM X

Terce, Cycles B & D

JUBILÁTE *Dómino* omnis terra, psalmum dícite nómini eius: date glóriam laudi eius. — *Ps. 65:1-2*

Dícite Deo, quam terribília sunt ópera tua, Dómine: in multitúdine virtútis tuæ mentiéntur tibi inimíci tui. — *Ps. 65:3*

Omnis terra adóret te et psallat tibi: psalmum dicat nómini tuo. — *Ps. 65:4*

Veníte, audíte, et narrábo, omnes, qui timétis Deum: quanta fecit ánimæ meæ. — *Ps. 65:16*

Ad ipsum ore meo clamávi: et exaltávi sub lingua mea. — *Ps. 65:17*

Et exaudívit de templo sancto suo vocem meam: et clamor meus in conspéctu eius. — *Ps. 17:7*

Benedícite gentes Dóminum nostrum: et audítam fácite vocem laudis eius. — *Ps. 65:8*

Et benedicéntur in ipso omnes tribus terræ: omnes gentes magnificábunt eum. — *Ps. 71:17*

Benedíctus Dóminus, Deus Israël: qui facit mirabília solus. — *Ps. 71:18*

Et benedíctum nomen maiestátis eius in ætérnum: et replébitur maiestáte eius omnis terra. Fiat, fiat. — *Ps. 71:19*

PSALM XI

Sext, Cycles B & D

Ps. 19:2   MAY the Lord hear thee in the day of tribulation: may the Name of the God of Jacob protect thee.

Ps. 19:3   May He send thee help from the sanctuary: and defend thee out of Sion.

Ps. 19:4   Be mindful of all thy sacrifices: and may thy whole burnt-offering be made fat.

Ps. 19:5   Give thee according to thy own heart: and confirm all thy counsels.

Ps. 19:6   We will rejoice in thy salvation: and in the Name of our God we shall be exalted.

Ps. 19:7, I Jn. 4:9, Ps. 9:9   The Lord fulfill all thy petitions; now I know that *the Lord hath sent Jesus Christ* His Son: and will judge the people with justice.

Ps. 9:10-11   The Lord is become a refuge for the poor, a helper in due time of tribulation: let them trust in Thee who know Thy Name.

Ps. 143:1, Ps. 58:17   Blessed be the Lord my God: for Thou art become my support and refuge: in the day of my trouble.

Ps. 58:18   Unto Thee, O my helper, will I sing, for God is my defense: my God, my mercy.

PSALM XI

Sext, Cycles B & D

EXÁUDIAT te Dóminus in die tribulatiónis: prótegat te nomen Dei Iacob. *Ps. 19:2*
Mittat tibi auxílium de sancto: et de Sion tueátur te. *Ps. 19:3*

Memor sit omnis sacrifícii tui: et holocáustum tuum pingue fiat. *Ps. 19:4*
Tríbuat tibi secúndum cor tuum: et omne consílium tuum confírmet. *Ps. 19:5*
Lætábimur in salutári tuo: et in nómine Dómini Dei nostri magnificábimur. *Ps. 19:6*
Ímpleat Dóminus omnes petitiónes tuas; nunc cognóvi, quóniam misit Dóminus Iesum Christum Fílium suum: et iudicábit pópulos in iustítia. *Ps. 19:7, I Jn. 4:9, Ps. 9:9*
Et factus est Dóminus refúgium páuperi, adiútor in opportunitátibus, in tribulatióne: et sperent in te qui novérunt nomen tuum. *Ps. 9:10-11*
Benedíctus Dóminus Deus meus: quia factus est suscéptor meus et refúgium meum in die tribulatiónis meæ. *Ps. 143:1, Ps. 58:17*
Adiútor meus, tibi psallam, quia Deus suscéptor meus: Deus meus, misericórdia mea. *Ps. 58:18*

PSALM XII

None, Cycles B & D

Ps. 70:1   IN Thee, O Lord, have I hoped: let me never be put to confusion.

Ps. 70:2   Incline Thine ear unto me: and save me.

Ps. 70:3   Be Thou unto me, O God, a protector and a place of strength: that Thou mayest make me safe.

Ps. 70:5   For Thou art my patience, O Lord: my hope, O Lord, from my youth.

Ps. 70:6   By Thee have I been confirmed from the womb, from my mother's womb Thou art my protector: of Thee shall I continually sing.

Ps. 70:8   Let my mouth be filled with praise, that I may sing Thy glory: Thy greatness all the day long.

Ps. 68:17   Hear me, O Lord, for Thy mercy is kind: look upon me according to the multitude of Thy tender mercies.

Ps. 68:18   And turn not away Thy face from Thy servant: for I am in trouble, hear me speedily.

Ps. 143:1, Ps. 58:17   Blessed be the Lord my God, for Thou art become my support and refuge: in the day of my trouble.

Ps. 58:18   Unto Thee, O my helper, will I sing, for God is my defense: my God, my mercy.

PSALM XII

None, Cycles B & D

IN te, Dómine, sperávi, non confúndar in ætérnum: *Ps. 70:1*
in iustítia tua líbera me et éripe me.
Inclína ad me aurem tuam: et salva me. *Ps. 70:2*

Esto mihi in Deum protectórem et in locum muní- *Ps. 70:3*
tum: ut salvum me fácias.
Quóniam tu es patiéntia mea, Dómine: Dómine, spes *Ps. 70:5*
mea a iuventúte mea.
In te confirmátus sum ex útero, de ventre matris meæ *Ps. 70:6*
tu es protéctor meus: in cantátio mea semper.

Repleátur os meum laude, ut cantem glóriam tuam: *Ps. 70:8*
tota die magnitúdinem tuam.
Exáudi me, Dómine, quóniam benígna est misericór- *Ps. 68:17*
dia tua: secúndum multitúdinem miseratiónum
tuárum réspice in me.
Et ne avértas fáciem tuam a púero tuo: quóniam tríbu- *Ps. 68:18*
lor, velóciter exáudi me.
Benedíctus Dóminus, Deus meus, quia factus est sus- *Ps. 143:1,*
céptor meus: et refúgium meum in die tribulatiónis *Ps. 58:17*
meæ.
Adiútor meus, tibi psallam, quia Deus suscéptor meus: *Ps. 58:18*
Deus meus, misericórdia mea.

PSALM XIII

Compline, Cycle D

Ps. 12—Usquequo, Domine

HOW long, O Lord, wilt Thou forget me unto the end? How long dost Thou turn away from me?

How long shall I take counsels in my soul: sorrow in my heart all the day?

How long shall my enemy be exalted over me? Consider, and hear me, O Lord my God.

Enlighten my eyes that I never sleep in death: lest at any time my enemy say, I have prevailed against him.

They that trouble me rejoice when I am moved: but I have trusted in thy mercy.

My heart shall rejoice in thy salvation: I will sing to the Lord, who giveth me good things; I will sing to the name of the Lord most High.

PSALM XIII

Compline, Cycle D

Ps. 12—Usquequo, Domine

USQUEQUO, Dómine, obliviscéris me in finem?
Úsquequo avértis fáciem tuam a me?

Quámdiu ponam consília in ánima mea: dolórem in corde meo per diem?

Úsquequo exaltábitur inimícus meus super me? Réspice, et exáudi me, Dómine Deus meus.

Illúmina óculos meos, ne umquam obdórmiam in morte: nequándo dicat inimícus meus, Præválui advérsus eum.

Qui tríbulant me exsultábunt si motus fúero: ego autem in misericórdia tua sperávi.

Exsultábit cor meum in salutári tuo: cantábo Dómino qui bona tríbuit mihi; et psallam nómini Dómini altíssimi.

PSALM XIV

Lauds, Cycle D

Ps. 85:12, Ps. 85:17 — I WILL praise Thee, O Lord, *most Holy Father*, King of Heaven and earth: because Thou hast comforted me.

Ps. 24:5, Ps. 11:6 — Thou art God my Savior: I will deal confidently and will not fear.

Ps. 117:4 — The Lord is my strength and my praise: and is become my salvation.

Ex. 15:6, Ex. 15:7 — Thy right hand, O Lord, is magnified in strength, Thy right hand, O Lord, hath slain the enemy: and in the multitude of Thy glory Thou has put down Thy adversaries.

Ps. 68:33 — Let the poor see and rejoice: seek God and your soul shall live.

Ps. 68:35 — Let the heavens and the earth praise Him: the sea and everything that creepeth therein.

Ps. 68:36 — For God will save Sion: and the cities of Juda shall be built up.

Ps. 68:36 — And they shall dwell there: and acquire it by inheritance.

Ps. 68:37 — And the seed of His servants shall possess it: and they that love His Name shall dwell therein.

PSALM XIV
Lauds, Cycle D

CONFITÉBOR tibi, Dómine, *sanctíssime Pater*, Rex cæli et terræ: quóniam consolátus es me. *Ps. 85:12, Ps. 85:17*

Tu es Deus Salvátor meus: fiduciáliter agam et non timébo. *Ps. 24:5, Ps. 11:6*

Fortitúdo mea et laus mea Dóminus: et factus est mihi in salútem. *Ps. 117:4*

Déxtera tua, Dómine, magnificáta est in fortitúdine; déxtera tua, Dómine, percússit inimícum: et in multitúdine glóriæ tuæ deposuísti adversários meos. *Ex. 15:6, Ex. 15:7*

Vídeant páuperes et læténtur: quærite Deum, et vivet ánima vestra. *Ps. 68:33*

Laudent illum cæli et terra: mare et ómnia reptília in eis. *Ps. 68:35*

Quóniam Deus salvam fáciet Sion: et ædificabúntur civitátes Iudæ. *Ps. 68:36*

Et inhabitábunt ibi: et hereditáte acquírent eam. *Ps. 68:36*

Et semen servórum eius possidébit eam: et qui díligunt nomen eius, habitábunt in ea. *Ps. 68:37*

PSALM XV

All hours except Compline and Prime, Cycle C

Ps. 80:2, Ps. 46:2	REJOICE to God our helper: shout to *the Lord God, living and true*, with the voice of triumph.
Ps. 46:3	For the Lord is high, terrible: a great king over all the earth.
Ps. 73:12	*For the most holy Father of heaven,* our King before ages, *sent His Beloved Son from on high: and He was born of the Blessed Virgin, holy Mary.*
Ps. 88:27-28	He shall cry out to me, Thou art my Father: and I will make Him My Firstborn, high above the kings of the earth.
Ps. 41:9	In the daytime the Lord hath commanded His mercy: and a canticle to Him in the night.
Ps. 117:24	This is the day which the Lord hath made: let us rejoice and be glad in it.
Is. 9:6, Lk. 2:7	For the beloved and most holy Child has been given to us and born for us by the wayside: and laid in a manger because He had no room in at the inn.
Lk. 2:14	Glory to God in the highest: and on earth peace to men of good will.
Ps. 95:11-12	Let the heavens rejoice and the earth be glad, and let the sea be moved and the fulness thereof: the fields shall rejoice and all that are in them.
Ps. 95:1	Sing to Him a new canticle: sing to the Lord, all the earth.
Ps. 95:4	For the Lord is great and exceedingly to be praised: He is to be feared above all gods.
Ps. 95:7-8	Bring to the Lord, O you kindreds of the gentiles, bring to the Lord glory and honor: bring to the Lord glory unto His name.
Lk. 14:27, Jn. 19:17, 1 Pt. 2:21	*Bring your own bodies and bear His holy cross: and follow His most holy precepts even unto the end.*

PSALM XV

All hours except Compline and Prime, Cycle C

EXSULTÁTE Deo adiutóri nostro: iubiláte *Dómino Deo vivo et vero* in voce exsultatiónis. — *Ps. 80:2, Ps. 46:2*

Quóniam Dóminus excélsus, terríbilis: Rex magnus super omnem terram. — *Ps. 46:3*

Quia sanctíssimus Pater de cælo, Rex noster, ante sǽcula misit diléctum Fílium suum de alto: et natus fuit de beáta Vírgine sancta María. — *Ps. 73:12*

Ipse invocábit me, Pater meus es tu: et ego primogénitum ponam illum, excélsum præ régibus terræ. — *Ps. 88:27-28*

In illa die mandávit Dóminus Deus misericórdiam suam: et nocte cánticum eius. — *Ps. 41:9*

Hæc est dies, quam fecit Dóminus: exsultémus et lætémur in ea. — *Ps. 117:24*

Quia sanctíssimus puer diléctus datus est nobis et natus fuit pro nobis in via et pósitus in præsépio: quia non habébat locum in diversório. — *Is. 9:6, Lk. 2:7*

Glória in altíssimis Dómino Deo: et in terra pax homínibus bonæ voluntátis. — *Lk. 2:14*

Læténtur cæli et exsúltet terra, commoveátur mare et plenitúdo eius: gaudébunt campi et ómnia, quæ in eis sunt. — *Ps. 95:11-12*

Cantáte ei cánticum novum: cantáte Dómino omnes terra. — *Ps. 95:1*

Quóniam magnus Dóminus et laudábilis nimis: terríbilis est super omnes deos. — *Ps. 95:4*

Afférte Dómino pátriæ géntium, afférte Dómino glóriam et honórem: afférte Dómino glóriam nómini eius. — *Ps. 95:7-8*

Tóllite córpora vestra et baiuláte sanctam crucem eius: et sequímini usque in finem sanctíssima præcépta eius. — *Lk. 14:27, Jn. 19:17, 1 Pt. 2.21*

St. John
Philadelphia, Free Library of Philadelphia, 1945-65-4 (Collins Hours), fol. 27v.

The Passion of Our Lord Jesus Christ According to St. John

Jn. 18:1-40; 19:1-42

AT that time Jesus went forth with His disciples over the brook Cedron, where there was a garden, into which He entered with His disciples. And Judas also, who betrayed Him, knew the place: because Jesus had often resorted thither together with His disciples. Judas therefore having received a band of soldiers and servants from the chief priests and the Pharisees, cometh thither with lanterns and torches and weapons. Jesus therefore, knowing all things that should come upon Him, went forth and said to them: Whom seek ye? They answered him: Jesus of Nazareth. Jesus saith to them: I am He. And Judas also, who betrayed Him, stood with them. As soon therefore as He had said to them: I am He, they went backward and fell to the ground. Again therefore He asked them: Whom seek ye? And they said: Jesus of Nazareth. Jesus answered: I have told you that I am He. If therefore you seek Me, let these go their

IN illo témpore: Egréssus est Iesus cum discípulis suis trans torréntem Cedron, ubi erat hortus, in quem introívit ipse, et discípuli eius. Sciébat autem et Iudas, qui tradébat eum, locum: quia frequénter Iesus convénerat illuc cum discípulis suis. Iudas ergo cum accepísset cohórtem et a pontifícibus et pharisǽis minístros, venit illuc cum latérnis, et fácibus, et armis. Iesus ítaque sciens ómnia, quæ ventúra erant super eum, procéssit, et dixit eis: Quem quǽritis? Respondérunt ei: Iesum Nazarénum. Dicit eis Iesus: Ego sum. Stabat autem et Iudas, qui tradébat eum, cum ipsis. Ut ergo dixit eis: Ego sum: abiérunt retrórsum, et cecidérunt in terram. Iterum ergo interrogávit eos: Quem quǽritis? Illi autem dixérunt: Iesum Nazarénum. Respóndit Iesus: Dixi vobis, quia ego sum: si ergo me quǽritis, sínite hos abíre. Ut implerétur sermo, quem dixit: Quia quos dedísti mihi, non pérdidi ex eis quemquam. Simon ergo Petrus habens glá-

way: that the word might be fulfilled which He said: Of them whom Thou hast given Me, I have not lost any one. Then Simon Peter, having a sword, drew it and struck the servant of the high priest and cut off his right ear. And the name of the servant was Malchus. Jesus therefore said to Peter: Put up thy sword into the scabbard. The chalice which My Father hath given Me, shall I not drink it? Then the band and the tribune and the servants of the Jews took Jesus, and bound Him. And they led Him away to Annas first, for he was the father-in-law to Caiphas, who was the high priest of that year. Now Caiphas was he who had given the counsel to the Jews: That it was expedient that one man should die for the people.

And Simon Peter followed Jesus: and so did another disciple. And that disciple was known to the high priest and went in with Jesus into the court of the high priest. But Peter stood at the door without. The other disciple therefore, who was known to the high priest, went out and spoke to the portress and brought in Peter. The maid therefore that was portress, saith to Peter: Art not thou also one

dium edúxit eum: et percússit pontíficis servum: et abscídit aurículam eius déxteram. Erat autem nomen servo Malchus. Dixit ergo Iesus Petro: Mitte gládium tuum in vagínam. Cálicem, quem dedit mihi Pater, non bibam illum? Cohors ergo, et tribúnus, et minístri Iudæórum comprehendérunt Iesum, et ligavérunt eum: et adduxérunt eum ad Annam primum, erat enim socer Cáiphæ, qui erat póntifex anni illíus. Erat autem Cáiphas, qui consílium déderat Iudǽis: Quia éxpedit, unum hóminem mori pro pópulo.

Sequebátur autem Iesum Simon Petrus, et álius discípulus. Discípulus autem ille erat notus pontífici, et introívit cum Iesu in átrium pontíficis. Petrus autem stabat ad óstium foris. Exívit ergo discípulus álius, qui erat notus pontífici, et dixit ostiáriæ: et introdúxit Petrum. Dicit ergo Petro ancílla ostiária: Numquid et tu ex discípulis es hóminis istíus? Dicit ille: Non sum. Stabant autem servi, et minístri ad

of this man's disciples? He saith: I am not. Now the servants and ministers stood at a fire of coals, because it was cold, and warmed themselves. And with them was Peter also, standing, and warming himself. The high priest therefore asked Jesus of His disciples and of His doctrine. Jesus answered him: I have spoken openly to the world. I have always taught in the synagogue and in the temple, whither all the Jews resort: and in secret I have spoken nothing. Why askest thou me? Ask them who have heard what I have spoken unto them. Behold they know what things I have said. And when He had said these things, one of the servants standing by gave Jesus a blow, saying: Answerest Thou the high priest so? Jesus answered him: If I have spoken evil, give testimony of the evil; but if well, why strikest thou Me? And Annas sent Him bound to Caiphas the high priest. And Simon Peter was standing and warming himself. They said therefore to him: Art not thou also one of His disciples? He denied it and said: I am not. One of the servants of the high priest (a kinsman to him whose ear Peter cut off) saith to him: Did I not see thee in the

prunas, quia frigus erat, et calefaciébant se: erat autem cum eis et Petrus stans, et calefáciens se. Póntifex ergo interrogávit Iesum de discípulis suis, et de doctrína eius. Respóndit ei Iesus: Ego palam locútus sum mundo: ego semper dócui in synagóga, et in templo, quo omnes Iudǽi convéniunt: et in occúlto locútus sum nihil. Quid me intérrogas? Intérroga eos, qui audiérunt quid locútus sim ipsis: ecce hi sciunt quæ díxerim ego. Hæc autem cum dixísset, unus assístens ministrórum dedit álapam Iesu, dicens: Sic respóndes pontífici? Respóndit ei Iesus: Si male locútus sum, testimónium pérhibe de malo: si autem bene, quid me cædis? Et misit eum Annas ligátum ad Cáipham pontíficem. Erat autem Simon Petrus stans et calefáciens se. Dixérunt ergo ei: Numquid et tu ex discípulis eius es? Negávit ille, et dixit: Non sum. Dicit ei unus ex servis pontíficis, cognátus eius, cuius abscídit Petrus aurículam: Nonne ego te vidi in horto cum illo? Iterum ergo negávit Petrus: et statim gallus cantávit.

garden with Him? Again therefore Peter denied; and immediately the cock crew.

Then they led Jesus from Caiphas to the governor's hall. And it was morning; and they went not into the hall, that they might not be defiled, but that they might eat the Pasch. Pilate therefore went out to them, and said: What accusation bring you against this man? They answered and said to him: If He were not a malefactor, we would not have delivered Him up to thee. Pilate therefore said to them: Take Him you, and judge Him according to your law. The Jews therefore said to him: It is not lawful for us to put any man to death. That the word of Jesus might be fulfilled, which He said, signifying what death He should die. Pilate therefore went into the hall again and called Jesus and said to Him: Art Thou the King of the Jews? Jesus answered: Sayest thou this thing of thyself, or have others told it thee of Me? Pilate answered: Am I a Jew? Thine own nation and the chief priests have delivered Thee up to me. What hast Thou done? Jesus answered: My kingdom is not of this world. If My kingdom were of this world, My ser-

Addúcunt ergo Iesum a Cáipha in prætórium. Erat autem mane: et ipsi non introiérunt in prætórium, ut non contaminaréntur, sed ut manducárent Pascha. Exívit ergo Pilátus ad eos foras, et dixit: Quam accusatiónem affértis advérsus hóminem hunc? Respondérunt et dixérunt ei: Si non esset hic maleféctor, non tibi tradidissémus eum. Dixit ergo eis Pilátus: Accípite eum vos, et secúndum legem vestram iudicáte eum. Dixérunt ergo ei Iudǽi: Nobis non licet interfícere quemquam. Ut sermo Iesu implerétur, quem dixit, signíficans qua morte esset moritúrus. Introívit ergo íterum in prætórium Pilátus, et vocávit Iesum, et dixit ei: Tu es Rex Iudæórum? Respóndit Iesus: A temetípso hoc dicis, an álii dixérunt tibi de me? Respóndit Pilátus: Numquid ego Iudǽus sum? Gens tua, et pontífices tradidérunt me mihi: quid fecísti? Respóndit Iesus: Regnum meum non est de hoc mundo. Si ex hoc mundo esset regnum meum, minístri mei útique decertárent ut non tráderer Iudǽis: nunc autem regnum meum non est hinc. Dixit ítaque ei Pilátus: Ergo Rex es tu? Re-

vants would certainly strive that I should not be delivered to the Jews: but now My kingdom is not from hence. Pilate therefore said to Him: Art Thou a King then? Jesus answered: Thou sayest that I am a King. For this was I born, and for this came I into the world; that I should give testimony of the truth. Every one that is of the truth heareth My voice. Pilate saith to Him. What is truth? And when he had said this, he went out again to the Jews and saith to them: I find no cause in Him. But you have a custom that I should release one unto you at the Pasch. Will you, therefore, that I release unto you the King of the Jews? Then cried they all again, saying: Not this man, but Barabbas. Now Barabbas was a robber. Then therefore Pilate took Jesus and scourged Him. And the soldiers platting a crown of thorns, put it upon His head; and they put on Him a purple garment. And they came to Him and said: Hail, King of the Jews. And they gave Him blows. Pilate therefore went forth again and saith to them: Behold, I bring Him forth unto you; that you may know that I find no cause in Him. (Jesus therefore came forth, bearing the crown of thorns and the pur-

spóndit Iesus: Tu dicis quia Rex sum ego. Ego in hoc natus sum, et ad hoc veni in mundum, ut testimónium perhíbeam veritáti: omnis qui est ex veritáte, audit vocem meam. Dicit ei Pilátus: Quid est véritas? Et cum hoc dixísset, íterum exívit ad Iudæos, et dicit eis: Ego nullam invénio in eo causam. Est autem consuetúdo vobis ut unum dimíttam vobis in Pascha: vultis ergo dimíttam vobis Regem Iudæórum? Clamavérunt ergo rursum omnes, dicéntes: Non hunc, sed Barábbam. Erat autem Barábbas latro. Tunc ergo apprehéndit Pilátus Iesum, et flagellávit. Et mílites plecténtes corónam de spinis, imposuérunt cápiti eius: et veste purpúrea circumdedérunt eum. Et veniébant ad eum, et dicébant: Ave Rex Iudæórum. Et dabant ei álapas. Exívit ergo íterum Pilátus foras, et dixit eis: Ecce addúco vobis eum foras, ut cognoscátis, quia nullam invénio in eo causam. (Exívit ergo Iesus portans corónam spíneam, et purpúreum vestiméntum). Et dicit eis: Ecce homo. Cum ergo vidíssent eum pontifices et minístri, clamábant, dicéntes: Crucifíge, crucifíge eum. Dicit eis Pilátus: Accípite eum vos, et crucifígite: ego enim non invénio in eo causam. Respondé-

ple garment.) And he saith to them: Behold the Man. When the chief priests, therefore, and the servants had seen Him, they cried out, saying: Crucify Him, crucify Him. Pilate saith to them: Take Him you, and crucify Him; for I find no cause in Him. The Jews answered him: We have a law, and according the law He ought to die, because He made Himself the Son of God. When Pilate, therefore, had heard this saying, he feared the more. And he entered into the hall again; and he said to Jesus: Whence art Thou? But Jesus gave him no answer. Pilate therefore saith to Him: Speakest Thou not to me? Knowest Thou not that I have power to crucify Thee, and I have power to release Thee? Jesus answered: Thou shouldst not have any power against Me, unless it were given thee from above. Therefore, he that hath delivered Me to thee hath the greater sin. And from henceforth Pilate sought to release Him. But the Jews cried out, saying: If thou release this man, thou art not Caesar's friend. For whosoever maketh himself a king speaketh against Caesar. Now when Pilate had heard these words, he brought Jesus forth and sat down in

runt ei Iudǽi: Nos legem habémus, et secúndum legem debet mori, quia Fílium Dei se fecit. Cum ergo audísset Pilátus hunc sermónem, magis tímuit. Et ingréssus est prætórium íterum: et dixit ad Iesum: Unde es tu? Iesus autem respónsum non dedit ei. Dicit ergo ei Pilátus: Mihi non loquéris? Nescis quia potestátem hábeo crucifígere te, et potestátem hábeo dimíttere te? Respóndit Iesus: Non habéres potestátem advérsum me ullam, nisi tibi datum esset désuper. Proptérea, qui me trádidit tibi, maius peccátum habet. Et exínde quærébat Pilátus dimíttere eum. Iudǽi autem clamábant dicéntes: Si hunc dimíttis, non es amícus Cǽsaris. Omnis enim, qui se regem facit, contradícit Cǽsari. Pilátus autem cum audísset hos sermónes, addúxit foras Iesum, et sedit pro tribunáli, in loco, qui dícitur Lithóstrotos, hebráice autem Gábbatha. Erat autem Parascéve Paschæ, hora quasi sexta, et dicit Iudǽis: Ecce Rex vester. Illi autem clamábant: Tolle, tolle, crucifíge eum. Dicit eis Pilátus: Regem vestrum crucifígam? Respondérunt pontífices: Non habémus regem, nisi Cǽsarem. Tunc ergo trádidit eis illum ut crucifigerétur.

the judgment seat, in the place that is called Lithostrotos, and in Hebrew Gabbatha. And it was the Parasceve of the Pasch, about the sixth hour; and he saith to the Jews: Behold your King. But they cried out: Away with Him. Away with Him. Crucify Him. Pilate saith to them: Shall I crucify your King? The chief priests answered: We have no king but Caesar. Then, therefore, he delivered Him to them to be crucified.

And they took Jesus and led Him forth. And bearing His cross, He went forth to that place which is called Calvary but in Hebrew Golgotha; there they crucified Him, and with Him two others, one on each side and Jesus in the midst. And Pilate wrote a title also: and he put it upon the cross. And the writing was: Jesus of Nazareth, the King of the Jews. This title therefore many of the Jews did read, because the place where Jesus was crucified was nigh to the city. And it was written in Hebrew, in Greek, and in Latin. Then the chief priests of the Jews said to Pilate: Write not: The King of the Jews, but that He said: I am the King of the Jews. Pilate answered: What I have written, I have written. The soldiers there-

Suscepérunt autem Iesum, et eduxérunt. Et báiulans sibi crucem, exívit in eum, qui dícitur Calváriæ locum, hebráice autem Gólgotha: ubi crucifixérunt eum, et cum eo álios duos, hinc et hinc, médium autem Iesum. Scripsit autem et títulum Pilátus: et pósuit super crucem. Erat autem scriptum: Iesus Nazarénus, Rex Iudæórum. Hunc ergo títulum multi Iudæórum legérunt, quia prope civitátem erat locus, ubi crucifíxus est Iesus. Et erat scriptum hebráice, græce, et latíne. Dicébant ergo Piláto pontífices Iudæórum: Noli scríbere, Rex Iudæórum, sed quia ipse dixit: Rex sum Iudæórum. Respóndit Pilátus: Quod scripsi, scripsi. Mílites ergo cum crucifixíssent eum, accepérunt vestiménta eius (et fecérunt

fore, when they had crucified Him, took His garments (and they made four parts, to every soldier a part) and also his coat. Now the coat was without seam, woven from the top throughout. They said then one to another: Let us not cut it, but let us cast lots for it, whose it shall be: that the Scripture might be fulfilled which saith: They have parted My garments among them, and upon My vesture they have cast lots. And the soldiers indeed did these things. Now there stood by the cross of Jesus His Mother, and His Mother's sister, Mary of Cleophas, and Mary Magdalen. When Jesus therefore had seen His Mother and the disciple standing whom He loved, He saith to His Mother: Woman, behold thy son. After that, He saith to the disciple: Behold thy mother. And from that hour, the disciple took her to his own. Afterwards, Jesus knowing that all things were now accomplished, that the Scripture might be fulfilled, said: I thirst. Now there was a vessel set there, full of vinegar. And they, putting a sponge full of vinegar about hyssop, put it to His mouth. Jesus therefore, when He had taken the vinegar, said: It is consummated. And quátuor partes: unicuíque míliti partem), et túnicam. Erat autem túnica inconsútilis, désuper contéxta per totum. Dixérunt ergo ad ínvicem: Non scindámus eam, sed sortiámur de illa cuius sit. Ut Scriptúra implerétur, dicens: Partíti sunt vestiménta mea sibi: et in vestem meam misérunt sortem. Et mílites quidem hæc fecérunt. Stabant autem iuxta crucem Iesu, mater eius, et soror matris eius María Cléophæ, et María Magdaléne. Cum vidísset ergo Iesus matrem, et discípulum stantem, quem diligébat, dicit matri suæ: Múlier, ecce fílius tuus. Deínde dicit discípulo: Ecce mater tua. Et ex illa hora accépit eam discípulus in sua. Póstea sciens Iesus quia ómnia consummáta sunt, ut consummarétur Scriptúra, dixit: Sítio. Vas ergo erat pósitum acéto plenum. Illi autem spóngiam plenam acéto, hyssópo circumponéntes, obtulérunt ori eius. Cum ergo accepísset Iesus acétum, dixit: Consummátum est. Et inclináto cápite trádidit spíritum.

bowing His head, He gave up the ghost.

Then the Jews (because it was the Parasceve), that the bodies might not remain upon the cross on the Sabbath day (for that was a great Sabbath day), besought Pilate that their legs might be broken and that they might be taken away. The soldiers therefore came, and they broke the legs of the first, and of the other that was crucified with Him. But after they were come to Jesus, when they saw that He was already dead, they did not break His legs. But one of the soldiers with a spear opened His side, and immediately there came out blood and water. And he that saw it hath given testimony: and his testimony is true. And he knoweth that he saith true: that you also may believe. For these things were done that the Scripture might be fulfilled: You shall not break a bone of Him. And again another Scripture saith: They shall look on Him Whom they pierced. And after these things Joseph of Arimathea (because he was a disciple of Jesus, but secretly for fear of the Jews) besought Pilate that he might take away the Body of Jesus. And Pilate gave leave. He came therefore and took away

Iudǽi ergo (quóniam Parascéve erat) ut non remanérent in cruce córpora sábbato (erat enim magnus dies ille sábbati), rogavérunt Pilátum, ut frangeréntur eórum crura, et tolleréntur. Venérunt ergo mílites: et primi quidem fregérunt crura, et altérius, qui crucifíxus est cum eo. Ad Iesum autem, cum veníssent, ut vidérunt eum iam mórtuum, non fregérunt eius crura: sed unus mílitum láncea latus eius apéruit, et contínuo exívit sanguis, et aqua. Et qui vidit, testimónium perhíbuit: et verum est testimónium eius. Et ille scit, quia vera dicit: ut et vos credátis. Facta sunt enim hæc, ut Scriptúra implerétur: Os non comminuétis ex eo. Et íterum ália Scriptúra dicit: Vidébunt in quem transfixérunt. Post hæc autem rogávit Pilátum Ioseph ab Arimathǽa (eo quod esset discípulus Iesu, occúltus autem propter metum Iudæórum), ut tólleret corpus Iesu. Et permísit Pilátus. Venit ergo, et tulit corpus Iesu. Venit autem et Nicodémus, qui vénerat ad Iesum nocte primum, ferens mixtúram myrrhæ, et áloës, quasi libras centum. Accepérunt ergo corpus Iesu, et ligavérunt illud

the Body of Jesus. And Nicodemus also came (he who at the first came to Jesus by night), bringing a mixture of myrrh and aloes, about a hundred pound weight. They took therefore the Body of Jesus and bound it in linen cloths, with the spices, as the manner of the Jews is to bury. Now there was in the place where He was crucified a garden: and in the garden a new sepulcher, wherein no man yet had been laid. There, therefore, because of the Parasceve of the Jews, they laid Jesus because the sepulcher was nigh at hand.

línteis cum aromátibus, sicut mos est Iudǽis sepelíre. Erat autem in loco, ubi crucifíxus est, hortus: et in horto monuméntum novum, in quo nondum quisquam pósitus erat. Ibi ergo propter Parascéven Iudæórum, quia iuxta erat monuméntum, posuérunt Iesum.

Tu es omnia divitia ad sufficientiam.
Tu es pulchritudo. Tu es mansuetudo.
Thou art all riches to sufficiency.
Thou art beauty. Thou art meekness.

St. Luke
Philadelphia, Free Library of Philadelphia, 1945-65-4 (Collins Hours), fol. 29v.

The Passion of Our Lord Jesus Christ According to St. Luke

Lk. 22:39-71; 23:1-53

AT that time, going out, Jesus went according to His custom to the Mount of Olives. And His disciples also followed Him. And when He was come to the place, He said to them: Pray, lest ye enter into temptation. And He was withdrawn away from them a stone's cast: and kneeling down, He prayed, saying: Father, if Thou wilt, remove this chalice from Me; but yet not My will, but Thine be done. And there appeared to Him an Angel from heaven, strengthening Him. And being in an agony, He prayed the longer. And His sweat became as drops of blood, trickling down upon the ground. And when He rose up from prayer, and was come to His disciples, He found them sleeping for sorrow. And He said to them: Why sleep you? arise, pray, lest you enter into temptation.

As He was yet speaking, behold a multitude; and he that was called Judas, one of the twelve, went before them, and drew near to Jesus for to kiss Him. And Jesus said to him: Judas, dost thou betray the

IN illo témpore: Egréssus Iesus ibat secúndum consuetúdinem in montem Olivárum. Secúti sunt autem illum et discípuli. Et cum pervenísset ad locum, dixit illis: Oráte, ne intrétis in tentatiónem. Et ipse avúlsus est ab eis quantum iactus est lápidis, et pósitis génibus orábat, dicens: Pater, si vis, transfer cálicem istum a me: verúmtamen non mea volúntas, sed tua fiat. Appáruit autem illi Angelus de cœlo, confórtans eum. Et factus in agónia, políxius orábat. Et factus est sudor eius, sicut guttæ sánguinis decurréntis in terram. Et cum surrexísset ab oratióne, et venísset ad discípulos suos, invénit eos dormiéntes præ tristítia. Et ait illis: Quid dormítis? súrgite, oráte, ne intrétis in tentatiónem.

Adhuc eo loquénte, ecce turba: et qui vocabátur Iudas, unus de duódecim, antecedébat eos: et appropinquávit Iesu, ut oscularétur eum. Iesus autem dixit illi: Iuda, ósculo Fílium hóminis tradis? Vidéntes autem hi, qui

Son of man with a kiss? And they that were about Him, seeing what would follow, said to Him: Lord, shall we strike with the sword? And one of them struck the servant of the high priest and cut off his right ear. But Jesus answering, said: Suffer ye thus far. And when He had touched his ear, He healed him. And Jesus said to the chief priests and magistrates of the temple and the ancients, that were come unto Him: Are ye come out as it were against a thief, with swords and clubs? When I was daily with you in the temple, you did not stretch forth your hands against Me: but this is your hour, and the power of darkness.

And apprehending Him, they led Him to the high priest's house; but Peter followed afar off. And when they had kindled a fire in the midst of the hall and were sitting about it, Peter was in the midst of them. Whom when a certain servant maid had seen sitting at the light and had earnestly beheld him, she said: This man also was with Him. But he denied Him, saying: Woman, I know Him not. And after a little while, another seeing him said: Thou also art one of them. But Peter said: O man, I am not. And

circa ipsum erant, quod futúrum erat, dixérunt ei: Dómine, si percútimus in gládio? Et percússit unus ex illis servum príncipis sacerdótum, et amputávit aurículam eius déxteram. Respóndens autem Iesus ait: Sínite usque huc. Et cum tetigísset aurículam eius, sanávit eum. Dixit autem Iesus ad eos, qui vénerant ad se, príncipes sacerdótum, et magistrátus templi, et senióres: Quasi ad latrónem exístis cum gládiis, et fústibus? Cum quotídie vobíscum fúerim in templo, non extendístis manus in me: sed hæc est hora vestra, et potéstas tenebrárum.

Comprehendéntes autem eum, duxérunt ad domum príncipis sacerdótum: Petrus vero sequebátur a longe. Accénso autem igne in médio átrii, et circumsedéntibus illis, erat Petrus in médio eórum. Quem cum vidísset ancílla quædam sedéntem ad lumen, et eum fuísset intúita, dixit: Et hic cum illo erat. At ille negávit eum, dicens: Múlier, non novi illum. Et post pusíllum álius videns eum dixit: Et tu de illis es. Petrus vero ait: O homo, non sum. Et intervállo facto quasi horæ uníus, álius

after the space as it were of one hour, another certain man affirmed, saying: Of a truth this man was also with Him, for he is also a Galilean. And Peter said: Man, I know not what thou sayest. And immediately, as he was yet speaking, the cock crew. And the Lord turning looked on Peter. And Peter remembered the word of the Lord, as He had said: Before the cock crow, thou shalt deny Me thrice. And Peter going out, wept bitterly. And the men that held Him mocked Him and struck Him. And they blindfolded Him and smote His face. And they asked Him, saying: Prophesy, who is it that struck Thee? And blaspheming, many other things they said against Him.

And as soon as it was day, the ancients of the people, and the chief priests and scribes came together, and they brought Him into their council, saying: If Thou be the Christ, tell us. And He saith to them: If I shall tell you, you will not believe Me: and if I shall also ask you, you will not answer Me, nor let Me go. But hereafter the Son of man shall be sitting on the right hand of the power of God. Then said they all: Art Thou then the Son of God? Who said: You say that I am. And they said: What need

quidam affirmábat, dicens: Vere et hic cum illo erat: nam et Galilǽus est. Et ait Petrus: Homo, néscio quid dicis. Et contínuo adhuc illo loquénte cantávit gallus. Et convérsus Dóminus respéxit Petrum. Et recordátus est Petrus verbi Dómini, sicut díxerat: Quia priúsquam gallus cantet, ter me negábis. Et egréssus foras Petrus flevit amáre. Et viri, qui tenébant illum, illudébant ei, cædéntes. Et velavérunt eum, et percutiébant fáciem eius et interrogábant eum, dicéntes: Prophetíza, quis est, qui te percússit? Et ália multa blasphemántes dicébant in eum.

Et ut factus est dies, convenérunt senióres plebis, et príncipes sacerdótum, et scribæ, et duxérunt illum in concílium suum, dicéntes: Si tu es Christus, dic nobis. Et ait illis: Si vobis díxero, non credétis mihi: si autem et interrogávero, non respondébitis mihi, neque dimittétis. Ex hoc autem erit Fílius hóminis sedens a dextris virtútis Dei. Dixérunt autem omnes: Tu ergo es Fílius Dei? Qui ait: Vos dícitis, quia ego sum. At illi dixérunt: Quid adhuc desiderámus testimónium? Ipsi enim audívimus

we any further testimony? For we ourselves have heard it from His own mouth. And the whole multitude of them, rising up, led Him to Pilate. And they began to accuse Him, saying: We have found this man perverting our nation, and forbidding to give tribute to Caesar, and saying that He is Christ the King. And Pilate asked Him, saying: Art Thou the King of the Jews? But He answering, said: Thou sayest it. And Pilate said to the chief priests and to the multitudes: I find no cause in this man. But they were more earnest, saying: He stirreth up the people, teaching throughout all Judea, beginning from Galilee to this place. And Pilate hearing Galilee, asked if the man were of Galilee. And when he understood that He was of Herod's jurisdiction, he sent Him away to Herod, who was also himself at Jerusalem in those days.

And Herod, seeing Jesus, was very glad: for he was desirous of a long time to see Him, because he had heard many things of Him: and he hoped to see some sign wrought by Him. And he questioned Him in many words. But He answered him nothing. And the chief priests and the scribes stood by, earnestly ac-

de ore eius. Et surgens omnis multitúdo eórum, duxérunt illum ad Pilátum. Cœpérunt autem illum accusáre, dicéntes: Hunc invénimus subverténtem gentem nostram, et prohibéntem tribúta dare Cǽsari, et dicéntem se Christum regem esse. Pilátus autem interrogávit eam, dicens: Tu es Rex Iudæórum? At ille respóndens, ait: Tu dicis. Ait autem Pilátus ad príncipes sacerdótum, et turbas: Nihil invénio causæ in hoc hómine. At illi invalescébant, dicéntes: Cómmovet pópulum, docens per univérsam Iudǽam, incípiens a Galilǽa usque huc. Pilátus autem áudiens Galilǽam, interrogávit si homo Galilǽus esset. Et ut cognóvit quod de Heródis potestáte esset, remísit eum ad Heródem, qui et ipse Ierosólymis erat illis diébus.

Heródes autem viso Iesu gavísus est valde. Erat enim cúpiens ex multo témpore vidére eum, eo quod audiérat multa de eo, et sperábat signum áliquod vidére ab eo fíeri. Interrogábat autem eum multis sermónibus. At ipse nihil illi respondébat. Stabant autem príncipes sacerdótum, et scribæ constánter

cusing Him. And Herod with his army set Him at nought and mocked Him, putting on Him a white garment, and sent Him back to Pilate. And Herod and Pilate were made friends that same day: for before they were enemies one to another.

And Pilate, calling together the chief priests and the magistrates and the people, said to them: You have presented unto me this man as one that perverteth the people, and behold I, having examined Him before you, find no cause in this man in those things wherein you accuse Him. No, nor Herod neither: for I sent you to him, and behold, nothing worthy of death is done to Him. I will chastise Him therefore and release Him. Now of necessity he was to release unto them one upon the feast day. But the whole multitude together cried out, saying: Away with this man, and release unto us Barabbas. Who for a certain sedition made in the city, and for a murder, was cast into prison. And Pilate again spoke to them, desiring to release Jesus. But they cried again, saying: Crucify Him, crucify Him. And he said to them the third time: Why, what evil hath this man done? I find no cause of death in Him:

accusántes eum. Sprevit autem illum Heródes cum exércitu suo: et illúsit indútum veste alba, et remísit ad Pilátum. Et facti sunt amíci Heródes et Pilátus in ipsa die: nam ántea inimíci erant ad ínvicem.

Pilátus autem convocátis princípibus sacerdótum et magistrátibus, et plebe, dixit ad illos: Obtulístis mihi hunc hóminem, quasi averténtem pópulum, et ecce ego coram vobis intérrogans, nullam causam invéni in hómine isto ex his, in quibus eum accusátis. Sed neque Heródes: nam remísi vos ad illum, et ecce nihil dignum morte actum est ei. Emendátum ergo illum dimíttam. Necésse autem habébat dimíttere eis per diem festum, unum. Exclamávit autem simul univérsa turba, dicens: Tolle hunc, et dimítte nobis Barábbam. Qui erat propter seditiónem quamdam factam in civitáte, et homicídium, missus in cárcerem. Iterum autem Pilátus locútus est ad eos, volens dimíttere Iesum. At illi succlamábant, dicéntes: Crucifíge, crucifíge eum. Ille autem tértio dixit ad illos: Quid enim mali fecit iste? Nullam causam mortis invénio in eo: corrípiam ergo illum, et dimíttam. At illi instábant vóci-

I will chastise Him therefore and let Him go. But they were instant with loud voices, requiring that He might be crucified. And their voices prevailed. And Pilate gave sentence that it should be as they required. And he released unto them him who for murder and sedition had been cast into prison, whom they had desired: but Jesus he delivered up to their will.

And as they led Him away, they laid hold of one Simon of Cyrene, coming from the country; and they laid the cross on him to carry after Jesus. And there followed Him a great multitude of people and of women, who bewailed and lamented Him. But Jesus turning to them, said: Daughters of Jerusalem, weep not over Me, but weep for yourselves and for your children. For behold, the days shall come wherein they will say: Blessed are the barren, and the wombs that have not borne, and the paps that have not given suck. Then shall they begin to say to the mountains: Fall upon us; and to the hills: Cover us. For if in the green wood they do these things, what shall be done in the dry? And there were also two other malefactors led with Him to be put to death. And when they were come to the place which is called

bus magnis, postulántes ut crucifigerétur. Et invalescébant voces eórum. Et Pilátus adiudicávit fíeri petitiónem eórum. Dimísit autem illis eum, qui propter homicídium et seditiónem missus fúerat in cárcerem, quem petébant: Iesum vero trádidit voluntáti eórum.

Et cum dúcerent eum, apprehendérunt Simónem quemdam Cyrenénsem, veniéntem de villa: et imposuérunt illi crucem portáre post Iesum. Sequebátur autem illum multa turba pópuli, et mulíerum, quæ plangébant, et lamentabántur eum. Convérsus autem ad illas Iesus dixit: Fíliæ Ierúsalem, nolíte flere super me, sed super vos ipsas flete, et super fílios vestros. Quóniam ecce vénient dies, in quibus dicent: Beátæ stériles, et ventres, qui non genuérunt, et úbera, quæ non lactavérunt. Tunc incípient dícere móntibus: Cádite super nos; et cóllibus: Operíte nos. Quia si in víridi ligno hæc fáciunt, in árido quid fiet? Ducebántur autem et álii duo nequam cum eo, ut interficeréntur. Et postquam venérunt in locum, qui vocátur Calváriæ, ibi crucifixérunt eum: et latrónes, unum a dextris, et álterum a sinístris. Iesus autem

Calvary, they crucified Him there: and the robbers, one on the right hand, and the other on the left. And Jesus said: Father, forgive them, for they know not what they do. But they, dividing His garments, cast lots. And the people stood beholding, and the rulers with them derided Him, saying: He saved others; let Him save Himself, if He be Christ, the Elect of God. And the soldiers also mocked Him, coming to Him and offering Him vinegar, and saying: If Thou be the King of the Jews, save Thyself. And there was also a superscription written over Him in letters of Greek and Latin, and Hebrew: This is the King of the Jews.

And one of those robbers who were hanged blasphemed Him, saying: If Thou be Christ, save Thyself and us. But the other answering, rebuked him, saying: Neither dost thou fear God, seeing thou art under the same condemnation? And we indeed justly, for we receive the due rewards of our deeds; but this man hath done no evil. And he said to Jesus: Lord, remember me when Thou shalt come into Thy kingdom. And Jesus said to him: Amen I say to thee: This day thou shalt be with Me in paradise.

dicébat: Pater, dimítte illis: non enim sciunt quid fáciunt. Dividéntes vero vestiménta eius, misérunt sortes. Et stabat pópulus spectans, et deridébant eum príncipes cum eis, dicéntes: Alios salvos fecit: se salvum fáciat, si hic est Christus Dei eléctus. Illudébant autem ei et mílites accedéntes, et acétum offeréntes ei, et dicéntes: Si tu es Rex Iudæórum, salvum te fac. Erat autem et superscríptio scripta super eum lítteris græcis, et latínis, et hebráicis: Hic est Rex Iudæórum.

Unus autem de his, qui pendébant, latrónibus, blasphemábat eum, dicens: Si tu es Christus, salvum fac temetípsum, et nos. Respóndens autem alter increpábat eum, dicens: Neque tu times Deum, quod in eádem damnatióne es. Et nos quidem iuste, nam digna factis recípimus; hic vero nihil mali gessit. Et dicébat ad Iesum: Dómine, meménto mei, cum véneris in regnum tuum. Et dixit illi Iesus: Amen dico tibi: Hódie mecum eris in paradíso.

And it was almost the sixth hour; and there was darkness over all the earth until the ninth hour. And the sun was darkened; and the veil of the temple was rent in the midst. And Jesus, crying with a loud voice, said: Father, into Thy hands I commend My spirit. And saying this, He gave up the ghost.

Now the centurion seeing what was done, glorified God, saying: Indeed this was a just man. And all the multitude of them that were come together to that sight and saw the things that were done, returned striking their breasts. And all His acquaintance and the women that had followed Him from Galilee stood afar off, beholding these things.

And behold there was a man named Joseph, who was a counselor, a good and a just man (the same had not consented to their counsel and doings), of Arimathea, a city of Judea, who also himself looked for the kingdom of God. This man went to Pilate and begged the body of Jesus. And taking Him down, he wrapped Him in fine linen and laid Him in a sepulcher that was hewed in stone, wherein never yet any man had been laid.

Erat autem fere hora sexta, et ténebræ factæ sunt in univérsam terram usque in horam nonam. Et obscurátus est sol: et velum templi scissum est médium. Et clamans voce magna Iesus, ait: Pater, in manus tuas comméndo spíritum meum. Et hæc dicens, exspirávit.

Videns autem centúrio quod factum fúerat, glorificávit Deum, dicens: Vere hic homo iustus erat. Et omnis turba eórum, qui simul áderant ad spectáculum istud, et vidébant quæ fiébant, percutiéntes péctora sua revertebántur. Stabant autem omnes noti eius a longe, et mulíeres, quæ secútæ eum erant a Galilǽa, hæc vidéntes.

Et ecce vir nómine Ioseph, qui erat decúrio, vir bonus, et iustus: hic non consénserat consílio, et áctibus eórum, ab Arimathǽa civitáte Iudǽæ, qui exspectábat et ipse regnum Dei. Hic accéssit ad Pilátum, et pétiit corpus Iesu: et depósitum invólvit síndone, et pósuit eum in monuménto excíso, in quo nondum quisquam pósitus fúerat.

Tu es protector. Tu es custos et defensor. Tu es fortitudo.
Thou art protector. Thou art guardian
and defender. Thou art strength.

St. Matthew
Philadelphia, Free Library of Philadelphia, 1945-65-4 (Collins Hours), fol. 32v.

The Passion of Our Lord Jesus Christ According to St. Matthew

Mt. 26:36-75; 27:1-60

AT that time Jesus came with them into a country place which is called Gethsemani; and He said to His disciples: Sit you here, till I go yonder and pray. And taking with Him Peter and the two sons of Zebedee, He began to grow sorrowful and to be sad. Then He saith to them: My soul is sorrowful even unto death; stay you here and watch with Me.

And going a little further, He fell upon His face, praying and saying: My Father, if it be possible, let this chalice pass from Me: nevertheless, not as I will, but as Thou wilt. And He cometh to His disciples, and findeth them asleep. And He saith to Peter: What! Could you not watch one hour with Me? Watch ye, and pray that ye enter not into temptation. The spirit indeed is willing, but the flesh is weak. Again the second time, He went and prayed, saying: My Father, if this chalice may not pass away, but I must drink it, Thy will be done. And He cometh again, and findeth them sleeping, for their eyes were heavy. And leaving them, He went again, and He prayed

IN illo témpore: venit Iesus cum discípulis suis in villam, quæ dícitur Gethsémani, et dixit discípulis suis: Sedéte hic, donec vadam illuc, et orem. Et assúmpto Petro, et duóbus fíliis Zebedǽi, cœpit contristári et mœstus esse. Tunc ait illis: Tristis est ánima mea usque ad mortem: sustinéte hic, et vigiláte mecum.

Et progréssus pusíllum, prócidit in fáciem suam, orans, et dicens: Pater mi, si possíbile est, tránseat a me calix iste. Verúmtamen non sicut ego volo, sed sicut tu. Et venit ad discípulos suos, et invénit eos dormiéntes: et dicit Petro: Sic non potuístis una hora vigiláre mecum? Vigiláte, et oráte, ut non intrétis in tentatiónem. Spíritus quidem promptus est, caro autem infirma. Iterum secúndo ábiit, et orávit, dicens: Pater mi, si non potest hic calix transíre, nisi bibam illum, fiat volúntas tua. Et venit íterum, et invénit eos dormiéntes: erant enim óculi eórum graváti. Et relíctis illis, íterum ábiit, et orávit tértio, eúmdem sermónem dicens.

the third time, saying the self-same word. Then He cometh to His disciples, and saith to them: Sleep ye now and take your rest; behold, the hour is at hand, and the Son of man shall be betrayed into the hands of sinners. Rise, let us go: behold, he is at hand that will betray Me.

As He yet spoke, behold Judas, one of the twelve, came, and with him a great multitude with swords and clubs, sent from the chief priests and the ancients of the people. And he that betrayed Him gave them a sign, saying: Whomsoever I shall kiss, that is He; hold Him fast. And forthwith coming to Jesus, he said: Hail, Rabbi. And he kissed Him. And Jesus said to him: Friend, whereto art thou come?

Then they came up and laid hands on Jesus, and held Him. And behold one of them that were with Jesus, stretching forth his hand, drew out his sword, and striking the servant of the High Priest, cut off his ear. Then Jesus saith to him: Put up again Thy sword into its place; for all that take the sword shall perish with the sword. Thinkest thou that I cannot ask My Father, and He will give Me presently more than twelve legions of Angels? How then shall the Scriptures be

Tunc venit ad discípulos suos, et dicit illis: Dormíte iam, et requiéscite: ecce appropinquávit hora, et Fílius hóminis tradétur in manus peccatórum. Súrgite, eámus: ecce appropinquávit qui me tradet.

Adhuc eo loquénte, ecce Iudas unus de duódecim venit, et cum eo turba multa cum gládiis et fústibus, missi a princípibus sacerdótum, et senióribus pópuli. Qui autem trádidit eum, dedit illis signum, dicens: Quemcúmque osculátus fúero, ipse est, tenéte eum. Et conféstim accédens ad Iesum, dixit: Ave, Rabbi. Et osculátus est eum. Dixítque illi Iesus: Amíce, ad quid venísti?

Tunc accessérunt, et manus iniecérunt in Iesum, et tenuérunt eum. Et ecce unus ex his, qui erant cum Iesu, exténdens manum, exémit gládium suum, et percútiens servum príncipis sacerdótum, amputávit aurículam eius. Tunc ait illi Iesus: Convérte gládium tuum in locum suum. Omnes enim, qui accéperint gládium, gládio períbunt. An putas, quia non possum rogáre Patrem meum, et exhibébit mihi modo plus quam duódecim legiónes Angelórum?

fulfilled, that so it must be done? In that same hour Jesus said to the multitudes: You are come out, as it were to a robber, with swords and clubs to apprehend Me. I sat daily with you, teaching in the Temple, and you laid not hands on Me. Now all this was done that the Scriptures of the Prophets might be fulfilled. Then the disciples, all leaving Him, fled.

But they holding Jesus, led Him to Caiphas the High Priest, where the scribes and the ancients were assembled. And Peter followed Him afar off, even to the court of the High Priest. And going in, he sat with the servants, that he might see the end. And the chief priests and the whole council sought false witness against Jesus, that they might put Him to death. And they found not, whereas many false witnesses had come in. And last of all there came two false witnesses; and they said: This man said, I am able to destroy the temple of God, and after three days to rebuild it. And the High Priest, rising up, said to Him: Answerest Thou nothing to the things which these witness against Thee? But Jesus held His peace. And the High Priest said to Him: I adjure Thee by the living God,

Quómodo ergo implebúntur Scriptúræ, quia sic opórtet fíeri? In illa hora dixit Iesus turbis: Tamquam ad latrónem exístis cum gládiis, et fústibus comprehéndere me: quotídie apud vos sedébam docens in templo, et non me tenuístis. Hoc autem totum factum est, ut adimpleréntur Scriptúræ prophetárum. Tunc discípuli omnes, relícto eo, fugérunt.

At illi tenéntes Iesum, duxérunt ad Cáipham príncipem sacerdótum, ubi scribæ et senióres convénerant. Petrus autem sequebátur eum a longe, usque in átrium príncipis sacerdótum. Et ingréssus intro, sedébat cum minístris, ut vidéret finem. Príncipes autem sacerdótum, et omne concílium, quærébant falsum testimónium contra Iesum, ut eum morti tráderent: et non invenérunt, cum multi falsi testes accessíssent. Novíssime autem venérunt duo falsi testes, et dixérunt: Hic dixit: Possum destrúere templum Dei, et post tríduum reædificáre illud. Et surgens princeps sacerdótum, ait illi: Nihil respóndes ad ea, quæ isti advérsum te testificántur? Iesus autem tacébat. Et princeps sacerdótum ait illi: Adiúro te per Deum vivum, ut dicas nobis, si tu es Christus Fí-

that Thou tell us if Thou be the Christ the Son of God. Jesus saith to him: Thou hast said it. Nevertheless I say to you, hereafter you shall see the Son of man sitting on the right hand of the power of God, and coming upon the clouds of heaven. Then the High Priest rent his garments, saying: He hath blasphemed; what further need have we of witnesses? Behold, now you have heard the blasphemy. What think you? But they answering said: He is guilty of death. Then did they spit in His face and buffeted Him: and others struck His face with the palms of their hands, saying: Prophesy unto us, O Christ, who is he that struck Thee?

But Peter sat without in the court, and there came to him a servant-maid, saying: Thou also wast with Jesus the Galilean. But he denied before them all, saying: I know not what thou sayest. And as he went out of the gate, another maid saw him, and she said to them that were there: This man also was with Jesus of Nazareth. And again he denied with an oath: I know not the man. And after a little while, they came that stood by and said to Peter: Surely thou also art one of them, for even thy speech doth discover thee. Then he began to curse and

lius Dei. Dicit illi Iesus: Tu dixísti. Verúmtamen dico vobis, ámodo vidébitis Fílium hóminis sedéntem a dextris virtútis Dei, et veniéntem in núbibus cœli. Tunc princeps sacerdótum scidit vestiménta sua, dicens: Blasphemávit: quid adhuc egémus téstibus? Ecce nunc audístis blasphémiam: quid vobis vidétur? At illi respondéntes dixérunt: Reus est mortis. Tunc exspuérunt in fáciem eius, et cólaphis eum cecidérunt, álii autem palmas in fáciem eius dedérunt, dicéntes: Prophetíza nobis, Christe, quis est qui te percússit?

Petrus vero sedébat foris in átrio: et accéssit ad eum una ancílla, dicens: Et tu cum Iesu Galilǽo eras. At ille negávit coram ómnibus, dicens: Néscio quid dicis. Exeúnte autem illo iánuam, vidit eum ália ancílla, et ait his, qui erant ibi: Et hic erat cum Iesu Nazaréno. Et íterum negávit cum iuraménto: Quia non novi hóminem. Et post pusíllum accessérunt qui stabant, et dixérunt Petro: Vere et tu ex illis es: nam et loquéla tua maniféstum te facit. Tunc cœpit detestári, et iuráre quia non novísset hóminem. Et contínuo

The Passion According to St. Matthew

to swear that he knew not the man; and immediately the cock crew. And Peter remembered the word of Jesus which He had said: Before the cock crow, thou wilt deny Me thrice. And going forth, he wept bitterly.

And when morning was come, all the chief priests and ancients of the people took counsel against Jesus, that they might put Him to death. And they brought Him bound, and delivered Him to Pontius Pilate the governor. Then Judas, who betrayed Him, seeing that He was condemned, repenting himself, brought back the thirty pieces of silver to the chief priests and ancients, saying: I have sinned in betraying innocent blood. But they said: What is that to us? Look thou to it. And casting down the pieces of silver in the Temple, he departed, and went and hanged himself with a halter. But the chief priests having taken the pieces of silver, said: It is not lawful to put them into the corbona, because it is the price of blood. And after they had consulted together, they bought with them the potter's field, to be a burying-place for strangers. For this cause that field was called Haceldama, that is, the field of blood, even to this day. Then was fulfilled that which was spoken

gallus cantávit. Et recordátus est Petrus verbi Iesu, quod díxerat: Priúsquam gallus cantet, ter me negábis. Et egréssus foras, flevit amáre.

Mane autem facto, concílium iniérunt omnes príncipes sacerdótum, et senióres pópuli advérsus Iesum, ut eum morti tráderent. Et vinctum adduxérunt eum, et tradidérunt Póntio Piláto præsidi. Tunc videns Iudas, qui eum trádidit, quod damnátus esset: pœniténtia ductus, rétulit trigínta argénteos princípibus sacerdótum, et senióribus, dicens: Peccávi, tradens sánguinem iustum. At illi dixérunt: Quid ad nos? Tu víderis. Et proiéctis argénteis in templo, recéssit: et ábiens, láqueo se suspéndit. Príncipes autem sacerdótum, accéptis argénteis, dixérunt: Non licet eos míttere in córbonam: quia prétium sánguinis est. Consílio autem ínito, emérunt ex illis agrum fíguli, in sepultúram peregrinórum. Propter hoc vocátus est ager ille, Hacéldama, hoc est, ager sánguinis, usque in hodiérnum diem. Tunc implétum est, quod dictum est per Ieremíam prophétam, dicéntem: Et accepérunt trigínta argénteos prétium

by Jeremias the prophet, saying: And they took the thirty pieces of silver, the price of Him that was prized, Whom they prized of the children of Israel; and they gave them unto the potter's field, as the Lord appointed to me.

And Jesus stood before the governor, and the governor asked Him, saying: Art Thou the King of the Jews? Jesus saith to him: Thou sayest it. And when He was accused by the chief priests and ancients, He answered nothing. Then Pilate saith to Him: Dost not Thou hear how great testimonies they allege against Thee? And He answered to him never a word, so that the governor wondered exceedingly.

Now upon the solemn day the governor was accustomed to release to the people one prisoner, whom they would. And he had then a notorious prisoner that was called Barabbas. They therefore being gathered together, Pilate said: Whom will you that I release to you: Barabbas, or Jesus that is called Christ? For he knew that for envy they had delivered Him. And as he was sitting in the place of judgment his wife sent to him, saying: Have thou nothing to do with that just man, for I have suffered many things this day in a dream

appretiáti, quem appretiavérunt a fíliis Israël: et dedérunt eos in agrum fíguli, sicut constítuit mihi Dóminus.

Iesus autem stetit ante præsidem, et interrogávit eum præses, dicens: Tu es Rex Iudæórum? Dicit illi Iesus: Tu dicis. Et cum accusarétur a princípibus sacerdótum, et senióribus, nihil respóndit. Tunc dicit illi Pilátus: Non audis quanta advérsum te dicunt testimónia? Et non respóndit ei ad ullum verbum, ita ut mirarétur præses veheménter.

Per diem autem solémnem consuéverat præses pópulo dimíttere unum vinctum, quem voluíssent. Habébat autem tunc vinctum insígnem, qui dicebátur Barábbas. Congregátis ergo illis, dixit Pilátus: Quem vultis dimíttam vobis: Barábbam, an Iesum, qui dícitur Christus? Sciébat enim quod per invídiam tradidíssent eum. Sedénte autem illo pro tribunáli, misit ad eum uxor eius, dicens: Nihil tibi et iusto illi: multa enim passa sum hódie per visum propter eum. Príncipes autem sacerdótum, et senióres persuasérunt pópulis,

because of Him. But the chief priests and ancients persuaded the people that they should ask Barabbas, and make Jesus away. And the governor answering, said to them: Whether will you of the two to be released unto you? But they said: Barabbas. Pilate saith to them: What shall I do then with Jesus that is called Christ? They say all: Let Him be crucified. The governor said to them: Why, what evil hath He done? But they cried out the more, saying: Let Him be crucified. And Pilate seeing that he prevailed nothing, but that rather a tumult was made, taking water washed his hands before the people, saying: I am innocent of the blood of this just man; look you to it. And the whole people answering, said: His blood be upon us and upon our children. Then he released to them Barabbas: and having scourged Jesus, delivered Him unto them to be crucified.

Then the soldiers of the governor, taking Jesus into the hall, gathered together unto Him the whole band; and stripping Him they put a scarlet cloak about Him. And platting a crown of thorns they put it upon His head and a reed in His right hand. And bowing the knee before Him, they mocked Him, saying: Hail,

ut péterent Barábbam, Iesum vero pérderent. Respóndens autem præses ait illis: Quem vultis vobis de duóbus dimítti? At illi dixérunt: Barábbam. Dicit illis Pilátus: Quid ígitur fáciam de Iesu, qui dícitur Christus? Dicunt omnes: Crucifigátur. Ait illis præses: Quid enim mali fecit? At illi magis clamábant, dicéntes: Crucifigátur. Videns autem Pilátus quia nihil profíceret, sed magis tumúltus fíeret: accépta aqua, lavit manus coram pópulo, dicens: Innocens ego sum a sánguine iusti huius: vos vidéritis. Et respóndens univérsus pópulus, dixit: Sanguis eius super nos, et super fílios nostros. Tunc dimísit illis Barábbam: Iesum autem flagellátum trádidit eis, ut crucifigerétur.

Tunc mílites præsidis suscipiéntes Iesum in prætórium, congregavérunt ad eum univérsam cohórtem: et exuéntes eum, chlámydem coccíneam circumdedérunt ei: et plecténtes corónam de spinis, posuérunt super caput eius, et arúndinem in déxtera eius. Et genu flexo ante eum, illudébant ei, dicéntes:

King of the Jews. And spitting upon Him, they took the reed and struck His head. And after they had mocked Him, they took off the cloak from Him, and put on Him His own garments, and led Him away to crucify Him.

And going out, they found a man of Cyrene, named Simon; him they forced to take up His cross. And they came to the place that is called Golgotha, which is the place of Calvary. And they gave Him wine to drink mingled with gall. And when He had tasted He would not drink. And after they had crucified Him, they divided His garments, casting lots; that it might be fulfilled which was spoken by the prophet, saying: They divided My garments among them, and upon My vesture they cast lots. And they sat and watched Him. And they put over His head His cause written: This is Jesus the King of the Jews. Then were crucified with Him two thieves: one on the right hand and one on the left. And they that passed by blasphemed Him, wagging their heads, and saying: Vah, Thou that destroyest the temple of God and in three days dost rebuild it, save Thine own self. If Thou be the Son of God, come down from the cross. In like manner also the chief

Ave, Rex Iudæórum. Et exspuéntes in eum, accepérunt arúndinem, et percutiébant caput eius. Et postquam illusérunt ei, exuérunt eum chlámyde, et induérunt eum vestiméntis eius, et duxérunt eum ut crucifígerent.

Exeúntes autem, invenérunt hóminem Cyrenæum, nómine Simónem: hunc angariavérunt, ut tólleret crucem eius. Et venérunt in locum qui dícitur Gólgotha, quod est Calváriæ locus. Et dedérunt ei vinum bíbere cum felle mixtum. Et cum gustásset, nóluit bíbere. Postquam autem crucifixérunt eum, divisérunt vestiménta eius, sortem mitténtes: ut implerétur, quod dictum est per prophétam, dicéntem: Divisérunt sibi vestiménta mea, et super vestem meam misérunt sortem. Et sedéntes, servábant eum. Et imposuérunt super caput eius causam ipsíus scriptam: Hic est Iesus Rex Iudæórum. Tunc crucifíxi sunt cum eo duo latrónes: unus a dextris, et unus a sinístris. Prætereúntes autem blasphemábant eum, movéntes cápita sua et dicéntes: Vah, qui déstruis templum Dei, et in tríduo illud reædíficas: salva temetípsum. Si Fílius Dei es, descénde de cruce. Simíliter et príncipes sacerdótum illudéntes cum scribis et senióribus, dicé-

The Passion According to St. Matthew

priests with the scribes and ancients, mocking, said: He saved others, Himself He cannot save; if He be the king of Israel, let Him now come down from the cross, and we will believe Him; He trusted in God, let Him now deliver Him if He will have Him; for He said: I am the Son of God. And the self-same thing the thieves also that were crucified with Him reproached Him with.

Now from the sixth hour there was darkness over the whole earth, until the ninth hour. And about the ninth hour, Jesus cried with a loud voice, saying: Eli, Eli, lamma sabacthani? That is: My God, My God, why hast Thou forsaken Me? And some that stood there and heard said: This man calleth Elias. And immediately one of them running took a sponge and filled it with vinegar and put it on a reed and gave Him to drink. And the others said: Let be; let us see whether Elias will come to deliver Him. And Jesus again crying with a loud voice, yielded up the ghost.

And behold the veil of the temple was rent in two from the top even to the bottom; and the earth quaked and the rocks were rent; and the graves were opened, and many bodies of the saints that had slept arose, and com-

bant: Alios salvos fecit, seípsum non potest salvum fácere: Si Rex Israël est, descéndat nunc de cruce, et crédimus ei: confídit in Deo: líberet nunc, si vult eum; dixit enim: Quia Fílius Dei sum. Idípsum autem et latrónes, qui crucifíxi erant cum eo, improperábant ei.

A sexta autem hora ténebræ factæ sunt super univérsam terram usque ad horam nonam. Et circa horam nonam clamávit Iesus voce magna, dicens: Eli, Eli, lamma sabactháni? Hoc est: Deus meus, Deus meus, ut quid dereliquísti me? Quidam autem illic stantes, et audiéntes, dicébant: Elíam vocat iste. Et contínuo currens unus ex eis, accéptam spóngiam implévit acéto, et impósuit arúndini, et dabat ei bíbere. Céteri vero dicébant: Sine, videámus an véniat Elías líberans eum. Iesus autem íterum clamans voce magna, emísit spíritum.

Et ecce velum templi scissum est in duas partes a summo usque deórsum: et terra mota est, et petræ scissæ sunt, et monuménta apérta sunt: et multa córpora sanctórum, qui dormíerant, surrexérunt. Et exeúntes

ing out of the tombs after His resurrection, came into the holy city, and appeared to many. Now the centurion and they that were with him watching Jesus, having seen the earthquake and the things that were done, were sore afraid, saying: Indeed this was the Son of God. And there were there many women afar off, who had followed Jesus from Galilee, ministering unto Him: among whom was Mary Magdalen, and Mary the mother of James and Joseph, and the mother of the sons of Zebedee.

And when it was evening, there came a certain rich man of Arimathea, named Joseph, who also himself was a disciple of Jesus. He went to Pilate and asked the body of Jesus. Then Pilate commanded that the body should be delivered. And Joseph taking the body wrapt it up in a clean linen cloth, and laid it in his own new monument, which he had hewed out in a rock. And he rolled a great stone to the door of the monument and went his way.

de monuméntis post resurrectiónem eius, venérunt in sanctam civitátem, et apparuérunt multis. Centúrio autem, et qui cum eo erant, custodiéntes Iesum, viso terræmótu, et his, quæ fiébant, timuérunt valde, dicéntes: Vere Fílius Dei erat iste. Erant autem ibi mulíeres multæ a longe, quæ secútæ erant Iesum a Galilǽa, ministrántes ei: inter quas erat María Magdaléne, et María Iacóbi et Ioseph mater, et mater filiórum Zebedǽi.

Cum autem sero factum esset, venit quidam homo dives ab Arimathǽa, nómine Ioseph, qui et ipse discípulus erat Iesu. Hic accéssit ad Pilátum, et pétiit corpus Iesu. Tunc Pilátus iussit reddi corpus. Et accépto córpore, Ioseph invólvit illud in síndone munda. Et pósuit illud in monuménto suo novo, quod excíderat in petra. Et advólvit saxum magnum ad óstium monuménti, et ábiit.

Tu es refrigerium. Tu es spes nostra.
Tu es fides nostra. Tu es magna dulcedo nostra.
Thou art refreshment. Thou art our hope.
Thou art our faith. Thou art our great sweetness.

St. Mark
Philadelphia, Free Library of Philadelphia, 1945-65-4 (Collins Hours), fol. 35v.

The Passion of Our Lord Jesus Christ According to St. Mark

Mk. 14:32-72; 15:1-46

AT that time Jesus and His disciples came to a farm called Gethsemani. And He said to His disciples: Sit you here while I pray. And He taketh Peter and James and John with Him, and He began to fear and to be heavy. And He saith to them: My soul is sorrowful even unto death; stay you here, and watch.

And when He was gone forward a little, He fell flat on the ground: and He prayed that, if it might be, the hour might pass from Him. And He saith: Abba, Father, all things are possible to Thee, remove this chalice from Me: but not what I will, but what Thou wilt. And He cometh and findeth them sleeping. And He saith to Peter: Simon, sleepest thou? Couldst thou not watch one hour? Watch ye, and pray that you enter not into temptation. The spirit indeed is willing, but the flesh is weak. And going away again, He prayed, saying the same words. And when He returned, He found them again asleep (for their eyes were heavy), and they knew not what to answer Him.

IN illo témpore: Iesus et discípuli eius véniunt in prædium, cui nomen Gethsémani. Et ait discípulis suis: Sedéte hic donec orem. Et assúmit Petrum et Iacóbum, et Ioánnem secum: et cœpit pavére, et tædére. Et ait illis Tristis est ánima mea usque ad mortem: sustinéte hic, et vigiláte.

Et cum processísset páululum, prócidit super terram, et orábat, ut si fíeri posset, transíret ab eo hora: et dixit: Abba, Pater, ómnia tibi possibília sunt, transfer cálicem hunc a me: sed non quod ego volo, sed quod tu. Et venit, et invénit eos dormiéntes. Et ait Petro: Simon, dormis? Non potuísti una hora vigiláre? Vigiláte, et oráte, ut non intrétis in tentatiónem. Spíritus quidem promptus est, caro vero infírma. Et íterum ábiens orávit, eúmdem sermónem dicens. Et revérsus, dénuo invénit eos dormiéntes (erant enim óculi eórum graváti) et ignorábant quid respondérent ei. Et venit tértio, et ait illis: Dormíte iam, et requiéscite. Súfficit: venit hora: ecce Fílius hóminis tradétur

And He cometh the third time and saith to them: Sleep ye now, and take your rest. It is enough: the hour is come: behold the Son of man shall be betrayed into the hands of sinners. Rise up: let us go. Behold he that will betray Me is at hand.

And while He was yet speaking, cometh Judas Iscariot, one of the twelve, and with him a great multitude with swords and staves, from the chief priests and the scribes and the ancients. And he that betrayed Him had given them a sign, saying: Whomsoever I shall kiss, that is He, lay hold on Him, and lead Him away carefully. And when he was come, immediately going up to Him, he saith: Hail, Rabbi! and he kissed Him. But they laid hands on Him and held Him. And one of them that stood by, drawing a sword, struck a servant of the chief priest and cut off his ear. And Jesus answering, said to them: Are you come out as to a robber, with swords and staves to apprehend Me? I was daily with you in the temple teaching, and you did not lay hands on Me. But that the Scriptures may be fulfilled. Then His disciples leaving Him, all fled away. And a certain young man followed Him, hav-

in manus peccatórum. Súrgite, eámus: ecce qui me tradet, prope est.

Et, adhuc eo loquénte, venit Iudas Iscariótes, unus de duódecim, et cum eo turba multa cum gládiis, et lignis, a summis sacerdótibus, et scribis, et senióribus. Déderat autem tráditor eius signum eis, dicens: Quemcúmque osculátus fúero, ipse est, tenéte eum, et dúcite caute. Et cum venísset, statim accédens ad eum, ait: Ave, Rabbi. Et osculátus est eum. At illi manus iniecérunt in eum, et tenuérunt eum. Unus autem quidam de circumstántibus, edúcens gládium, percússit servum summi sacerdótis: et amputávit illi aurículam. Et respóndens Iesus, ait illis: Tamquam ad latrónem exístis cum gládiis, et lignis comprehéndere me? Quotídie eram apud vos in templo docens, et non me tenuístis. Sed ut impleántur Scriptúræ. Tunc discípuli eius relinquéntes eum, omnes fugérunt. Adoléscens autem quidam sequebátur eum amíctus síndone super nudo: et tenuérunt eum. At ille, reiécta síndone, nudus profúgit ab eis.

ing a linen cloth cast about his naked body, and they laid hold on him. But he, casting off the linen cloth, fled from them naked.

And they brought Jesus to the high priest, and all the priests and the scribes and the ancients assembled together. And Peter followed Him afar off, even into the court of the high priest; and he sat with the servants at the fire and warmed himself. And the chief priests and all the council sought for evidence against Jesus, that they might put Him to death, and found none. For many bore false witness against Him, and their evidence did not agree. And some rising up, bore false witness against Him, saying: We heard Him say, I will destroy this temple made with hands, and within three days I will build another not made with hands. And their witness did not agree. And the high priest rising up in the midst, asked Jesus, saying: Answerest Thou nothing to the things that are laid to Thy charge by these men? But He held His peace and answered nothing. Again the high priest asked Him, and said to Him: Art thou the Christ, the Son of the Blessed God? And Jesus said

Et adduxérunt Iesum ad summum sacerdótem: et convenérunt omnes sacerdótes, et scribæ, et senióres. Petrus autem a longe secútus est eum usque intro in átrium summi sacerdótis: et sedébat cum minístris ad ignem, et calefaciébat se. Summi vero sacerdótes, et omne concílium, quærébant advérsus Iesum testimónium, ut eum morti tráderent, nec inveniébant. Multi enim testimónium falsum dicébant advérsus eum: et conveniéntia testimónia non erant. Et quidam surgéntes, falsum testimónium ferébant advérsus eum, dicéntes: Quóniam nos audívimus eum dicéntem: Ego dissólvam templum hoc manufáctum et per tríduum áliud non manufáctum ædificábo. Et non erat convéniens testimónium illórum. Et exsúrgens summus sacérdos in médium, interrogávit Iesum, dicens: Non respóndes quidquam ad ea, quæ tibi obiiciúntur ab his? Ille autem tacébat et nihil respóndit. Rursum summus sacérdos interrogábat eum, et dixit ei: Tu es Christus Fílius Dei benedícti? Iesus autem dixit

to him: I am. And you shall see the Son of man sitting on the right hand of the power of God, and coming with the clouds of heaven. Then the high priest, rending his garments, saith: What need we any further witnesses? You have heard the blasphemy. What think you? Who all condemned Him to be guilty of death. And some began to spit on Him, and to cover His face, and to buffet Him, and to say unto Him: Prophesy. And the servants struck Him with the palms of their hands.

Now when Peter was in the court below, there cometh one of the maid-servants of the high priest, and when she had seen Peter warming himself, looking on him, she saith: Thou also wast with Jesus of Nazareth. But he denied, saying: I neither know nor understand what thou sayest. And he went forth before the court, and the cock crew. And again a maid-servant seeing him began to say to the standers by: This is one of them. But he denied again. And after a while they that stood by said again to Peter: Surely thou art one of them, for thou art also a Galilean. But he began to curse and to swear, saying: I know not this man of whom you speak.

illi: Ego sum: et vidébitis Fílium hóminis sedéntem a dextris virtútis Dei, et veniéntem cum núbibus cœli. Summus autem sacérdos scindens vestiménta sua, ait: Quid adhuc desiderámus testes? Audístis blasphémiam: quid vobis vidétur? Qui omnes condemnavérunt cum esse reum mortis. Et cœpérunt quidam conspúere eum, et veláre fáciem eius, et cólaphis eum cædere, et dícere ei: Prophetíza. Et minístri álapis eum cædébant.

Et cum esset Petrus in átrio deórsum, venit una ex ancíllis summi sacerdótis: et cum vidísset Petrum calefaciéntem se, aspíciens illum, ait: Et tu cum Iesu Nazaréno eras. At ille negávit, dicens: Neque scio, neque novi quid dicas. Et éxiit foras ante átrium, et gallus cantávit. Rursus autem cum vidísset illum ancílla, cœpit dícere circumstántibus: Quia hic ex illis est. At ille íterum negávit. Et post pusíllum rursus qui astábant, dicébant Petro: Vere ex illis es: nam et Galilæus es. Ille autem cœpit anathematizáre, et iuráre: Quia néscio hóminem istum, quem dícitis. Et statim gallus íterum cantávit. Et recordátus est Petrus verbi, quod díxerat ei Iesus: Priúsquam

And immediately the cock crew again. And Peter remembered the word that Jesus had said unto him: Before the cock crow twice, thou shalt thrice deny Me. And he began to weep.

And straightway in the morning the chief priests holding a consultation with the ancients and the scribes and the whole council, binding Jesus, led Him away and delivered Him to Pilate.

And Pilate asked Him: Art Thou the King of the Jews? But He answering saith to him: Thou sayest it. And the chief priests accused Him in many things. And Pilate again asked Him, saying: Answerest Thou nothing? Behold in how many things they accuse Thee. But Jesus still answered nothing, so that Pilate wondered.

Now on the festival day he was wont to release unto them one of the prisoners, whomsoever they demanded. And there was one called Barabbas, who was put in prison with some seditious men, who in the sedition had committed murder. And when the multitude was come up, they began to desire that he would do as he had ever done unto them. And Pilate answered them, and said: Will you

gallus cantet bis, ter me negábis. Et cœpit flere.

Et conféstim mane consílium faciéntes summi sacerdótes, cum senióribus, et scribis, et univérso concílio, vinciéntes Iesum, duxérunt et tradidérunt Piláto.

Et interrogávit eum Pilátus: Tu es Rex Iudæórum? At ille respóndens, ait illi: Tu dicis. Et accusábant eum summi sacerdótes in multis. Pilátus autem rursum interrogávit eum, dicens: Non respóndens quidquam? vide in quantis te accúsant. Iesus autem ámplius nihil respóndit, ita ut mirarétur Pilátus.

Per diem autem festum solébat dimíttere illis unum ex vinctis, quemcúmque petiíssent. Erat autem qui dicebátur Barábbas, qui cum seditiósis erat vinctus, qui in seditióne fécerat homicídium. Et cum ascendísset turba, cœpit rogáre, sicut semper faciébat illis. Pilátus autem respóndit eis, et dixit: Vultis dimíttam vobis Regem Iudæórum? Sciébat enim quod per invídiam tradidíssent eum sum-

that I release to you the King of the Jews? For he knew that the chief priests had delivered Him up out of envy. But the chief priests moved the people, that he should rather release Barabbas to them. And Pilate again answering, saith to them: What will you then that I do to the King of the Jews? But they again cried out: Crucify Him. And Pilate saith to them: Why, what evil hath He done? But they cried out the more: Crucify Him. And so Pilate, wishing to satisfy the people, released to them Barabbas, and delivered up Jesus, when he had scourged Him, to be crucified.

And the soldiers led Him away into the court of the palace, and they called together the whole band: and they clothed Him with purple, and platting a crown of thorns, they put it upon Him. And they began to salute Him: Hail, King of the Jews. And they struck His head with a reed, and they did spit on Him, and bowing their knees they adored Him. And after they had mocked Him, they took off the purple from Him and put His own garments on Him, and they led Him out to crucify Him. And they forced one Simon a Cyrenian,

mi sacerdótes. Pontífices autem concitavérunt turbam, ut magis Barábbam dimítteret eis. Pilátus autem íterum respóndens, ait illis: Quid ergo vultis fáciam Regi Iudæórum? At illi íterum clamavérunt: Crucifíge eum. Pilátus vero dicébat illis: Quid enim mali fecit? At illi magis clamábant: Crucifíge eum. Pilátus autem volens pópulo satisfácere, dimísit illis Barábbam, et trádidit Iesum flagéllis cæsum, ut crucifigerétur.

Mílites autem duxérunt eum in átrium prætórii, et cónvocant totam cohórtem, et índuunt eum púrpura, et impónunt ei plecténtes spíneam corónam. Et cœpérunt salutáre eum: Ave, Rex Iudæórum. Et percutiébant caput eius arúndine: et conspuébant eum, et ponéntes génua, adorábant eum. Et postquam illusérunt ei, exuérunt illum púrpura, et induérunt eum vestiméntis suis: et edúcunt illum, ut crucifígerent eum. Et angariavérunt prætereúntem quémpiam, Simónem Cyrenæum, veniéntem de villa, patrem Alexándri, et Rufi, ut tólleret crucem eius.

who passed by coming out of the country, the father of Alexander and of Rufus, to take up His cross. And they bring Him into the place called Golgotha, which being interpreted is, the place of Calvary.

And they gave Him to drink wine mingled with myrrh: but He took it not. And crucifying Him they divided His garments, casting lots upon them, what every man should take. And it was the third hour, and they crucified Him. And the inscription bearing the charge against Him was: The King of the Jews. And with Him they crucify two thieves, the one on His right hand and the other on His left. And the Scripture was fulfilled which saith: And with the wicked He was reputed. And they that passed by, blasphemed Him, wagging their heads and saying: Vah, Thou that destroyest the temple of God and in three days buildest it up again, save Thyself, coming down from the cross. In like manner also the chief priests, mocking, said with the scribes one to another: He saved others, Himself He cannot save. Let Christ, the King of Israel, come down now from the cross, that we may see

Et perdúcunt illum in Gólgotha locum, quod est interpretátum Calváriæ locus.

Et dabant ei bíbere myrrhátum vinum: et non accépit. Et crucifigéntes eum, divisérunt vestiménta eius, mitténtes sortem super eis, quis quid tólleret. Erat autem hora tértia: et crucifixérunt eum. Et erat títulus causæ eius inscríptus: Rex Iudæórum. Et cum eo crucifígunt duos latrónes: unum a dextris, et álium a sinístris eius. Et impléta est Scriptúra, quæ dicit: Et cum iníquis reputátus est. Et prætereúntes blasphemábant eum, movéntes cápita sua, et dicéntes: Vah, qui déstruis templum Dei, et in tribus diébus reædíficas: salvum fac temetípsum, descéndens de cruce. Simíliter et summi sacerdótes illudéntes, ad altérutrum cum scribis dicébant: Alios salvos fecit, seípsum non potest salvum fácere. Christus Rex Israël descéndat nunc de cruce, ut videámus, et credámus. Et qui cum eo crucifíxi erant, convitiabántur ei.

and believe. And they that were crucified with Him reviled Him.

And when the sixth hour was come, there was darkness over the whole earth until the ninth hour. And at the ninth hour, Jesus cried out with a loud voice, saying: Eloi, Eloi, lamma sabacthani? which is, being interpreted: My God, My God, why hast Thou forsaken Me? And some of the standers-by hearing, said: Behold He calleth Elias. And one running and filling a sponge with vinegar and putting it upon a reed, gave Him to drink, saying: Stay, let us see if Elias come to take Him down. And Jesus, having cried out with a loud voice, gave up the ghost.

And the veil of the temple was rent in two, from the top to the bottom. And the centurion who stood over against Him, seeing that crying out in this manner He had given up the ghost, said: Indeed this man was the Son of God. And there were also women looking on afar off, among whom was Mary Magdalen, and Mary the mother of James the Less and of Joseph, and Salome; who also when He was in Galilee followed Him and ministered to Him, and many other women that came up with Him to Jerusalem. And when

Et facta hora sexta, ténebræ factæ sunt per totam terram, usque in horam nonam. Et hora nona exclamávit Iesus voce magna, dicens: Eloi, Eloi, lamma sabachtáni? Quod est interpretátum: Deus meus, Deus meus, ut quid dereliquísti me? Et quidam de circumstántibus audiéntes, dicébant: Ecce, Elíam vocat. Currens autem unus, et implens spóngiam acéto, circumponénsque cálamo, potum dabat ei, dicens: Sínite, videámus si véniat Elías ad deponéndum eum. Iesus autem emíssa voce magna exspirávit.

Et velum templi scissum est in duo, a summo usque deórsum. Videns autem centúrio, qui ex advérso stabat, quia sic clamans exspirásset, ait: Vere hic homo Fílius Dei erat. Erant autem et mulíeres de longe aspiciéntes: inter quas erat María Magdaléne, et María Iacóbi minóris, et Ioseph mater, et Salóme: et cum esset in Galilǽa, sequebántur eum, et ministrabant ei, et áliæ multæ, quæ simul cum eo ascénderant Ierosólymam. Et cum iam sero esset factum (quia erat Parascéve, quod est ante sábbatum) venit

evening was now come (because it was the Parasceve, that is the day before the Sabbath), Joseph of Arimathea, a noble counselor, who was also himself looking for the kingdom of God, came and went in boldly to Pilate and begged the Body of Jesus. But Pilate wondered that He should be already dead. And sending for the centurion, he asked him if He were already dead. And when he had understood it by the centurion, he gave the Body to Joseph. And Joseph, buying fine linen, and taking Him down, wrapped Him up in the fine linen and laid Him in a sepulcher which was hewed out of a rock, and he rolled a stone to the door of the sepulcher.

Ioseph ab Arimathǽa nóbilis decúrio, qui et ipse erat exspéctans regnum Dei, et audácter introívit ad Pilátum, et pétiit corpus Iesu. Pilátus autem mirabátur si iam obiísset. Et accersíto centurióne, interrogávit eum si iam mórtuus esset. Et cum cognovísset a centurióne, donávit corpus Ioseph. Ioseph autem mercátus síndonem, et depónens eum invólvit síndone et pósuit eum in monuménto, quod erat excísum de petra, et advólvit lápidem ad óstium monuménti.

The Seven Penitential Psalms

PSALM 6 *Domine, ne in furore tuo…miserere*

O LORD, rebuke me not in Thy indignation: nor chastise me in Thy wrath.

Have mercy on me, O Lord, for I am weak: heal me, O Lord, for my bones are troubled.

And my soul is troubled exceedingly: but Thou, O Lord, how long?

Turn to me, O Lord, and deliver my soul: O save me for Thy mercy's sake.

For there is no one in death, that is mindful of Thee: and who shall confess to Thee in hell?

I have laboured in my groanings, every night I will wash my bed: I will water my couch with my tears.

My eye is troubled through indignation: I have grown old amongst all my enemies.

Depart from me, all ye workers of iniquity: for the Lord hath heard the voice of my weeping.

The Lord hath heard my

DÓMINE, ne in furóre tuo árguas me: neque in ira tua corrípias me.

Miserére mei, Dómine, quóniam infírmus sum: sana me, Dómine, quóniam conturbáta sunt ossa mea.

Et ánima mea turbáta est valde: sed tu, Dómine, úsquequo?

Convértere, Dómine, et éripe ánimam meam: salvum me fac propter misericórdiam tuam.

Quóniam non est in morte qui memor sit tui: in inférno autem quis confitébitur tibi?

Laborávi in gémitu meo, lavábo per síngulas noctes lectum meum: lácrimis meis stratum meum rigábo.

Turbátus est a furóre óculus meus: inveterávi inter omnes inimícos meos.

Discédite a me omnes qui operámini iniquitátem: quóniam exaudívit Dóminus vocem fletus mei.

Exaudívit Dóminus depreca-

supplication: the Lord hath received my prayer.

Let all my enemies be ashamed, and be very much troubled: let them be turned back, and be ashamed very speedily.

tiónem meam, Dóminus oratiónem meam suscépit.

Erubéscant et conturbéntur veheménter omnes inimíci mei: convertántur et erubéscant valde velóciter.

PSALM 31 *Beati quorum*

BLESSED are they whose iniquities are forgiven, and whose sins are covered.

Blessed is the man to whom the Lord hath not imputed sin: and in whose spirit there is no guile.

Because I was silent my bones grew old: whilst I cried out all the day long.

For day and night Thy hand was heavy upon me: I am turned in my anguish, whilst the thorn is fastened.

I have acknowledged my sin to thee: and my injustice I have not concealed.

I said I will confess against myself my injustice to the Lord: and Thou hast forgiven the wickedness of my sin.

For this shall every one that is holy pray to Thee in a seasonable time: and yet in a flood of many waters, they shall not come nigh unto Him.

Thou art my refuge from the trouble which hath encom-

BEÁTI quorum remíssae sunt iniquitátes : * et quorum tecta sunt peccáta.

Beátus vir cui non imputávit Dóminus peccátum: nec est in spíritu eius dolus.

Quóniam tácui, inveteravérunt ossa mea: dum clamárem tota die.

Quóniam die ac nocte graváta est super me manus tua: convérsus sum in ærúmna mea, dum confígitur spina.

Delíctum meum cógnitum tibi feci: et iniustítiam meam non abscóndi.

Dixi: Confitébor advérsum me iniustítiam meam Dómino: et tu remisísti impietátem peccáti mei.

Pro hac orábit ad te omnis sanctus in témpore opportúno: verúmtamen in dilúvio aquárum multárum, ad eum non approximábunt.

Tu es refúgium meum a tribulatióne quæ circúmdedit me:

passed me: my joy, deliver me from them that surround me.

I will give thee understanding, and I will instruct thee in this way, in which thou shalt go: I will fix my eyes upon thee.

Do not become like the horse and the mule, who have no understanding: with bit and bridle bind fast their jaws, who come not near unto Thee.

Many are the scourges of the sinner: but mercy shall encompass him that hopeth in the Lord.

Be glad in the Lord, and rejoice, ye just: and glory, all ye right of heart.

exsultátio mea, érue me a circumdántibus me.

Intelléctum tibi dabo, et ínstruam te in via hac qua gradiéris: firmábo super te óculos meos.

Nolíte fíeri sicut equus et mulus, quibus non est intelléctus: in camo et freno maxíllas eórum constrínge, qui non appróximant ad te.

Multa flagélla peccatóris: sperántem autem in Dómino misericórdia circúmdabit.

Lætámini in Dómino, et exsultáte, iusti: et gloriámini, omnes recti corde.

PSALM 37 *Domine, ne in furore tuo…quoniam*

REBUKE me not, O Lord, in Thy indignation: nor chastise me in Thy wrath.

For Thy arrows are fastened in me: and Thy hand hath been strong upon me.

There is no health in my flesh, because of Thy wrath: there is no peace for my bones, because of my sins.

For my iniquities are gone over my head: and as a heavy burden are become heavy upon me.

My sores are putrified and corrupted: because of my foolishness.

DÓMINE, ne in furóre tuo árguas me: neque in ira tua corrípias me.

Quóniam sagíttæ tuæ infíxæ sunt mihi: et confirmásti super me manum tuam.

Non est sánitas in carne mea a fácie iræ tuæ: non est pax óssibus meis a fácie peccatórum meórum.

Quóniam iniquitátes meæ supergréssæ sunt caput meum: et sicut onus grave gravátæ sunt super me.

Putruérunt et corrúptæ sunt cicatríces meæ: a fácie insipiéntiæ meæ.

I am become miserable, and am bowed down even to the end: I walked sorrowful all the day long.

For my loins are filled with illusions: and there is no health in my flesh.

I am afflicted and humbled exceedingly: I roared with the groaning of my heart.

Lord, all my desire is before thee: and my groaning is not hidden from thee.

My heart is troubled, my strength hath left me: and the light of my eyes itself is not with me.

My friends and my neighbours have drawn near: and stood against me.

And they that were near me stood afar off: and they that sought my soul used violence.

And they that sought evils to me spoke vain things: and studied deceits all the day long.

But I, as a deaf man, heard not: and as a dumb man not opening his mouth.

And I became as a man that heareth not: and that hath no reproofs in his mouth.

For in Thee, O Lord, have I hoped: Thou wilt hear me, O Lord my God.

For I said: Lest at any time my enemies rejoice over me: and

Miser factus sum, et curvátus sum usque in finem: tota die contristátus ingrediébar.

Quóniam lumbi mei impléti sunt illusiónibus: et non est sánitas in carne mea.

Afflíctus sum, et humiliátus sum nimis: rugiébam a gémitu cordis mei.

Dómine, ante te omne desidérium meum: et gémitus meus a te non est abscónditus.

Cor meum conturbátum est, derelíquit me virtus mea: et lumen oculórum meórum, et ipsum non est mecum.

Amíci mei et próximi mei: advérsum me appropinquavérunt et stetérunt.

Et qui iuxta me erant de longe stetérunt: et vim faciébant qui quærébant ánimam meam.

Et qui inquirébant mala mihi, locúti sunt vanitátes: et dolos tota die meditabántur.

Ego autem tamquam surdus non audiébam: et sicut mutus non apériens os suum.

Et factus sum sicut homo non áudiens: et non habens in ore suo redargutiónes.

Quóniam in te, Dómine, sperávi: tu exáudies me, Dómine, Deus meus.

Quia dixi: Nequándo supergáudeant mihi inimíci mei: et

whilst my feet are moved, they speak great things against me.

For I am ready for scourges: and my sorrow is continually before me.

For I will declare my inequity: and I will think for my sin.

But my enemies live, and are stronger that I: and they hate me wrongfully are multiplied.

They that render evil for good, have detracted me: because I followed goodness.

Forsake me not, O Lord my God: do not Thou depart from me.

Attend unto my help, O Lord: the God of my salvation.

dum commovéntur pedes mei, super me magna locúti sunt.

Quóniam ego in flagélla parátus sum: et dolor meus in conspéctu meo semper.

Quóniam iniquitátem meam annuntiábo: et cogitábo pro peccáto meo.

Inimíci autem mei vivunt, et confirmáti sunt super me: et multiplicáti sunt qui odérunt me iníque.

Qui retríbuunt mala pro bonis, detrahébant mihi: quóniam sequébar bonitátem.

Ne derelínquas me, Dómine, Deus meus: ne discésseris a me.

Inténde in adiutórium meum: Dómine, Deus salútis meæ.

PSALM 50 *Miserere*

HAVE mercy on me, O God: according to Thy great mercy.

And according to the multitude of Thy tender mercies: blot out my iniquity.

Wash me yet more from my iniquity: and cleanse me from my sin.

For I know my iniquity: and my sin is always before me.

To Thee only have I sinned, and have done evil before Thee: that thou mayst be justified in

MISERÉRE mei, Deus: secúndum magnam misericórdiam tuam.

Et secúndum multitúdinem miseratiónum tuárum: dele iniquitátem meam.

Amplius lava me ab iniquitáte mea: et a peccáto meo munda me:

Quóniam iniquitátem meam ego cognósco: et peccátum meum contra me est semper.

Tibi soli peccávi, et malum coram te feci: ut iustificéris in sermónibus tuis, et vincas cum

thy words and mayst overcome when thou art judged.

For behold I was conceived in iniquities: and in sins did my mother conceive me.

For behold Thou hast loved truth: the uncertain and hidden things of Thy wisdom thou hast made manifest to me.

Thou shalt sprinkle me with hyssop, and I shall be cleansed: Thou shalt wash me, and I shall be made whiter than snow.

To my hearing Thou shalt give joy and gladness: and the bones that have been humbled shall rejoice.

Turn away Thy face from my sins: and blot out all my iniquities.

Create a clean heart in me, O God: and renew a right spirit within my bowels.

Cast me not away from thy face: and take not Thy Holy Spirit from me.

Restore unto me the joy of thy salvation: and strengthen me with a perfect spirit.

I will teach the unjust Thy ways: and the wicked shall be converted to Thee.

Deliver me from blood, O God, thou God of my salvation: and my tongue shall extol Thy justice.

iudicáris.

Ecce enim in iniquitátibus concéptus sum: et in peccátis concépit me mater mea.

Ecce enim veritátem dilexísti: incérta et occúlta sapiéntiæ tuæ manifestásti mihi.

Aspérges me hyssópo, et mundábor: lavábis me, et super nivem dealbábor.

Audítui meo dabis gáudium et lætítiam: et exsultábunt ossa humiliáta.

Avérte fáciem tuam a peccátis meis: et omnes iniquitátes meas dele.

Cor mundum crea in me, Deus: et spíritum rectum ínnova in viscéribus meis.

Ne proíicias me a fácie tua: et Spíritum Sanctum tuum ne áuferas a me.

Redde mihi lætítiam salutáris tui: et spíritu principáli confírma me.

Docébo iníquos vias tuas: et ímpii ad te converténtur.

Líbera me de sanguínibus, Deus, Deus, salútis meæ: et exsultábit lingua mea iustítiam tuam.

O Lord, Thou wilt open my lips: and my mouth shall declare Thy praise.

For if Thou hadst desired sacrifice, I would indeed have given it: with burnt offerings thou wilt not be delighted.

A sacrifice to God is an afflicted spirit: a contrite and humbled heart, O God, thou wilt not despise.

Deal favourably, O Lord, in Thy good will with Sion: that the walls of Jerusalem may be built up.

Then shalt Thou accept the sacrifice of justice, oblations and whole burnt offerings: then shall they lay calves upon Thy altar.

Dómine, lábia mea apéries: et os meum annuntiábit laudem tuam.

Quóniam si voluísses sacrifícium, dedíssem útique: holocáustis non delectáberis.

Sacrifícium Deo spíritus contribulátus: cor contrítum et humiliátum, Deus, non despícies.

Benígne fac, Dómine, in bona voluntáte tua Sion: ut ædificéntur muri Ierúsalem.

Tunc acceptábis sacrifícium iustítiæ, oblatiónes et holocáusta: tunc impónent super altáre tuum vítulos.

PSALM 101 *Domine, exaudi…et clamor meus*

HEAR, O Lord, my prayer: and let my cry come to Thee.

Turn not away Thy face from me: in the day when I am in trouble, incline Thy ear to me.

In what day soever I shall call upon Thee: hear me speedily.

For my days are vanished like smoke: and my bones are grown dry like fuel for the fire.

I am smitten as grass, and my heart is withered: because I forgot to eat my bread.

DÓMINE, exáudi oratiónem meam: et clamor meus ad te véniat.

Non avértas fáciem tuam a me: in quacúmque die tríbulor, inclína ad me aurem tuam;

In quacúmque die invocávero te: velóciter exáudi me.

Quia defecérunt sicut fumus dies mei: et ossa mea sicut crémium aruérunt.

Percússus sum ut fœnum, et áruit cor meum: quia oblítus sum comédere panem meum.

Through the voice of my groaning: my bone hath cleaved to my flesh.	A voce gémitus mei: adhǽsit os meum carni meæ.
I am become like to a pelican of the wilderness: I am like a night raven in the house.	Símilis factus sum pellicáno solitúdinis: factus sum sicut nyctícorax in domicílio.
I have watched: and am become as a sparrow all alone on the housetop.	Vigilávi: et factus sum sicut passer solitárius in tecto.
All the day long my enemies reproached me: and they that praised me did swear against me.	Tota die exprobrábant mihi inimíci mei: et qui laudábant me advérsum me iurábant.
For I did eat ashes like bread: and mingled my drink with weeping.	Quia cínerem tamquam panem manducábam: et potum meum cum fletu miscébam,
Because of thy anger and indignation: for having lifted me up thou hast thrown me down.	A fácie iræ et indignatiónis tuæ: quia élevans allisísti me.
My days have declined like a shadow: and I am withered like grass.	Dies mei sicut umbra declinavérunt: et ego sicut fœnum árui.
But Thou, O Lord, endurest for cvcr: and thy memorial to all generations.	Tu autem, Dómine, in ætérnum pérmanes: et memoriále tuum in generatiónem et generatiónem.
Thou shalt arise and have mercy on Sion: for it is time to have mercy on it, for the time is come.	Tu exsúrgens miseréberis Sion: quia tempus miseréndi eius, quia venit tempus:
For the stones thereof have pleased Thy servants: and they shall have pity on the earth thereof.	Quóniam placuérunt servis tuis lápides eius: et terræ eius miserebúntur.
And the Gentiles shall fear Thy name, O Lord: and all the kings of the earth Thy glory.	Et timébunt gentes nomen tuum, Dómine: et omnes reges terræ glóriam tuam.

For the Lord hath built up Sion: and He shall be seen in his glory.

He hath had regard to the prayer of the humble: and He hath not despised their petition.

Let these things be written unto another generation: and the people that shall be created shall praise the Lord:

Because He hath looked forth from His high sanctuary: from heaven the Lord hath looked upon the earth.

That He might hear the groans of them that are in fetters: that He might release the children of the slain:

That they may declare the name of the Lord in Sion: and His praise in Jerusalem;

When the people assemble together: and kings, to serve the Lord.

He answered him in the way of his strength: Declare unto me the fewness of my days.

Call me not away in the midst of my days: thy years are unto generation and generation.

In the beginning, O Lord, Thou foundedst the earth: and the heavens are the works of Thy hands.

They shall perish but Thou remainest: and all of them shall grow old like a garment: and as a

Quia ædificávit Dóminus Sion: et vidébitur in glória sua.

Respéxit in oratiónem humílium: et non sprevit precem eórum.

Scribántur hæc in generatióne áltera: et pópulus qui creábitur laudábit Dóminum.

Quia prospéxit de excélso sancto suo: Dóminus de cælo in terram aspéxit:

Ut audíret gémitus compeditórum: ut sólveret fílios interemptórum.

Ut annúntient in Sion nomen Dómini: et laudem eius in Ierúsalem;

In conveniéndo pópulos in unum: et reges, ut sérviant Dómino.

Respóndit ei in via virtútis suæ: Paucitátem diérum meórum núntia mihi.

Ne révoces me in dimídio diérum meórum: in generatiónem et generatiónem anni tui.

Inítio tu, Dómine, terram fundásti: et ópera mánuum tuárum sunt cæli.

Ipsi períbunt, tu autem pérmanes; et omnes sicut vestiméntum veteráscent: et sicut

vesture Thou shalt change them, and they shall be changed.

But Thou art always the selfsame: and Thy years shall not fail.

The children of Thy servants shall continue: and their seed shall be directed for ever.

opertórium mutábis eos, et mutabúntur.

Tu autem idem ipse es: et anni tui non defícient.

Fílii servórum tuórum habitábunt: et semen eórum in sǽculum dirigétur.

PSALM 129 *De profundis*

OUT of the depths I have cried to Thee, O Lord: Lord, hear my voice.

Let Thy ears be attentive: to the voice of my supplication.

If Thou, O Lord, wilt mark iniquities: Lord, who shall stand it?

For with Thee there is merciful forgiveness: and by reason of Thy law, I have waited for Thee, O Lord.

My soul hath relied on His word: my soul hath hoped in the Lord.

From the morning watch even until night: let Israel hope in the Lord.

Because with the Lord there is mercy: and with Him plentiful redemption.

And He shall redeem Israel: from all his iniquities.

DE profúndis clamávi ad te, Dómine: Dómine, exáudi vocem meam.

Fiant aures tuæ intendéntes: in vocem deprecatiónis meæ.

Si iniquitátes observáveris, Dómine: Dómine, quis sustinébit?

Quia apud te propitiátio est: et propter legem tuam sustínui te, Dómine.

Sustínuit ánima mea in verbo eius: sperávit ánima mea in Dómino.

A custódia matutína usque ad noctem: speret Israël in Dómino.

Quia apud Dóminum misericórdia: et copiósa apud eum redémptio.

Et ipse rédimet Israël: ex ómnibus iniquitátibus eius.

PSALM 142 *Domine, exaudi...auribus*

HEAR, O Lord, my prayer: give ear to my supplication in Thy truth: hear me in Thy justice.

And enter not into judgment with Thy servant: for in Thy sight no man living shall be justified.

For the enemy hath persecuted my soul: he hath brought down my life to the earth.

He hath made me to dwell in darkness as those that have been dead of old: and my spirit is in anguish within me: my heart within me is troubled.

I remembered the days of old, I meditated on all Thy works: I meditated upon the works of Thy hands.

I stretched forth my hands to Thee: my soul is as earth without water unto Thee.

Hear me speedily, O Lord: my spirit hath fainted away.

Turn not away Thy face from me: lest I be like unto them that go down into the pit.

Cause me to hear Thy mercy in the morning: for in Thee have I hoped.

Make the way known to me, wherein I should walk: for I have lifted up my soul to Thee.

DÓMINE exáudi oratiónem meam; áuribus pércipe obsecratiónem meam in veritáte tua: exáudi me in tua iustítia.

Et non intres in iudícium cum servo tuo: quia non iustificábitur in conspéctu tuo omnis vivens.

Quia persecútus est inimícus ánimam meam: humiliávit in terra vitam meam.

Collocávit me in obscúris, sicut mórtuos sǽculi: et anxiátus est super me spíritus meus; in me turbátum est cor meum.

Memor fui diérum antiquórum; meditátus sum in ómnibus opéribus tuis: in factis mánuum tuárum meditábar.

Expándi manus meas ad te: ánima mea sicut terra sine aqua tibi.

Velóciter exáudi me, Dómine: defécit spíritus meus.

Non avértas fáciem tuam a me: et símilis ero descendéntibus in lacum.

Audítam fac mihi mane misericórdiam tuam: quia in te sperávi.

Notam fac mihi viam in qua ámbulem: quia ad te levávi ánimam meam.

Deliver me from my enemies, O Lord, to Thee have I fled: teach me to do Thy will, for Thou art my God.

Thy good spirit shall lead me into the right land: for Thy name's sake, O Lord, Thou wilt quicken me in Thy justice.

Thou wilt bring my soul out of trouble: and in Thy mercy Thou wilt destroy my enemies.

And Thou wilt cut off all them that afflict my soul: for I am Thy servant.

Eripe me de inimícis meis, Dómine, ad te confúgi: doce me fácere voluntátem tuam, quia Deus meus es tu.

Spíritus tuus bonus dedúcet me in terram rectam: propter nomen tuum, Dómine, vivificábis me in æquitáte tua.

Edúces de tribulatióne ánimam meam: et in misericórdia tua dispérdes inimícos meos.

Et perdes omnes qui tríbulant ánimam meam: quóniam ego servus tuus sum.

Tu es vita aeterna nostra, magnus et admirabilis Dominus, Deus omnipotens, misericors Salvator.
Thou art our eternal life, great and admirable Lord, God Almighty, merciful Saviour.